Sue Sharpe was born in Londo ......
Girl, is about the developmen......
her research for a thesis on the......
in London secondary schools in the 1970s. This led to an
increasing interest in women and work and her next book,
Double Identity, focused on the lives of working mothers. She
became involved in the Women's Liberation Movement in
the early 1970s and worked in various areas of feminist
research and teaching. In 1980 she spent sixteen months
living and travelling in Mexico and Central America. In her
last book, *Falling For Love* (Virago Upstarts, 1987), she
explores the experience of teenage motherhood and all its
implications. She lives in London and works freelance, inter-
viewing and writing for books and magazines, and for a variety
of research projects.

VIRAGO UPSTARTS is a series of books for girls and young women. Upstarts are about love and romance, family and friends, work and school – and about new preoccupations – because in the last two decades the lives and expectations of girls have changed a lot. With fiction of all kinds – humour, mystery, love stories, science fiction, detective stories, thrillers – and nonfiction, these books show the funny, difficult and exciting real lives and times of teenage girls today. Lively, down-to-earth and entertaining, Virago's list is an important new Upstart on the scene.

VOICES FROM HOME

Girls Talk About Their Families

SUE SHARPE

VIRAGO

Published by Virago Press Limited 1990
20–23 Mandela Street, Camden Town, London NW1 0HQ

*A CIP Catalogue record for this book
is available from the British Library*

Typeset by CentraCet, Cambridge
Printed in Great Britain by
Cox and Wyman Ltd, Reading, Berks.

Contents

Contents

Acknowledgements

Many people helped to make this book, the most important of whom are the girls from many different parts of Britain who generously shared their thoughts, feelings, and personal experiences. I'd like to thank all of them warmly, particularly those whose voices speak throughout these pages, and also the many others who wrote to me at length about their families. Several people and organisations put me in contact with girls, and in particular I want to thank Julie Ibbott; Janet Jeffreys from the Alone in London Service; the National Council for One-Parent Families; and the magazines *Just Seventeen*, *Jackie* and *19*, a paragraph in whose pages produced such a great response. I'd like to express my gratitude to all those who provided a place to stay when I was travelling to do my interviews; to Sonia Lane, who deftly transcribed my tapes; to Jose Lees, who read and helpfully commented on the interviews; to Leah Drane, and Collette and Caroline Newton for advice on the chapter divisions; and special thanks to John Freeman for his invaluable help and support.

Introduction

The family is like a theatre whose stage provides the setting for drama and emotion – joy, conflict, closeness, tragedy, success, frustration, humour and love. The ideal family presents a rosy picture of mother, father and children all living happily ever after, but this is true only for some. For others the family can be a source of conflict and unhappiness. In many cases it has become more complicated through divorce and remarriage, or fragmented by an unforeseen tragedy such as illness or death. It won't conform to a neat, cosy unit. Family life starts on the day you are born. It can vary from moment to moment – sometimes it's good and other times it's hell – but it's still your family and whether you love it or hate it, the experiences are with you for life.

In this book, girls talk about life in their families, and it's very likely that somewhere within these pages their voices will echo your own. Many talk of love and co-operation, support and solidarity, while others chart angry clashes and sulky moods; some discuss the effects of their parents' divorce or remarriage; others describe living with poverty, drunkenness, death, violence and abuse. Each chapter of the book focuses on a different theme, and because family life is so intertwined, some girls could easily have gone into more than one chapter. For instance, a girl whose relationship with her mother forced her to leave could equally well appear in a chapter on mothers and one on leaving home. In the end, they each appear in the chapter they seem to illustrate the best.

The backgrounds, circumstances, and areas of the country they live in are as varied as their experiences. They contacted me after reading the requests I'd placed in magazines, asking if girls would share their family experiences with me. A few more I met through teachers. The response was enormous and I am really sorry that I have not been able to include everybody. I corresponded with over eighty girls, a third of whom I travelled to meet and talk to in more depth. Some felt free to meet me at their homes with the knowledge of their parents, but most preferred to meet and talk on more neutral territory, like a park, a coffee bar in Miss Selfridge, or a McDonald's. Some entertained me independently at university, at boarding school, or in a bedsit. I greatly enjoyed meeting and talking to them all, and I hope they enjoyed it too. I am privileged that they confided some of their most personal feelings and experiences to me, and to preserve anonymity their names have been changed throughout the book.

Family life constantly defies its ideal image, exploding the myth of the happy family into an array of changing shapes and patterns. The lives of many girls talking in this book contain a whole range of positive and negative elements – trust, openness, warmth and understanding rub shoulders with anger, conflict, rejection and loneliness. Their voices describe the experiences that are most significant for them at this time. Not surprisingly, a lot of them would like to change aspects of their family situation, while others take great comfort and security from it. Whatever its shape or pattern, family life, for all its faults, is very important. Many pay tribute to an enduring sense of loyalty and love, and despite difficulty and hardship they express great strength and determination.

1
Trust, Freedom and Equality

Having to tell lies: **Lai**
Because you're a girl: **Anna**
Wrapped in cotton wool: **Denise**

They think I'm being unreasonable and I think they're being unreasonable and it usually means one of us has got to get upset. Obviously they've got to have some rules but I think they go over the top. They hear so many things, they're frightened of anything happening to me. But I'm not stupid and I think they've got to let me find things out for myself.

Denise's resentment is running high as she tries to assert her right to freedom and independence. Although it seems easier today for girls to go to clubs and discos, or congregate down the pub, the sparks can still fly at home. Freedom can be a very touchy subject. Parents read the papers and assume that there's danger on every street. In the end it seems to come down to a question of trust, a trust that in Karen's view (in Chapter 10) goes both ways: 'It makes me feel a lot more responsible to be trusted, and I respect them a lot more for letting us out.'

Parents make the rules; sometimes these are mutually agreeable but often they're not. Many girls complained about lack of freedom and independence, and the conflict this caused at home. But while Denise's response was anger and frustration, some girls resolved the situation by lying to their parents. Lai feels guilty that she can't tell her parents the truth, but knows without asking that she wouldn't be allowed to go where she wants, and describes how deception is the only way.

In terms of freedom and independence, boys win hands down. As they are not as likely to be attacked and raped, they are generally allowed out more often and can come in later than girls. Parents are not so concerned to ferry them around, and worry about them far less. Anna's brother is younger than she is, but at sixteen, he is allowed to stay out later than she was at that age, and can drink what he wants. But this is not the only area where he's got it easier. Despite efforts to create more equality in men's and women's lives, and in the way boys and girls are brought up, boys get away with a lot at home. Parents still tend to expect daughters to look after younger brothers and sisters, and do more around the house. So they are less free within the home as well as outside it! Several girls complained strongly of this, including Anna, who keenly feels the effects of these and other differences in the way she and her brother are treated.

LAI

Lai is fifteen and lives in the London suburbs with her parents, who came here from Hong Kong with her two elder brothers. Her parents and uncle run a restaurant together, but her father's been ill and unable to work there much. Her brothers have left home, one to his own flat and the other to university, and she gets spoiled because she is the only girl. There aren't many other Chinese families living nearby; she has English friends at school, and speaks English everywhere except at home. Her parents let her go out, but not to the places she really wants to go, so she has to find ways round this. They are very generous with money, and she has just started working in a dry cleaner's, so she feels quite wealthy. She is hoping eventually to get enough exams to go to university.

'Mum has to work at the restaurant a bit in the evenings. Dad stays home most nights but he doesn't mind if I go out. I've got this Chinese friend who lives near me, who I've known since nursery school. They're family friends and I always say I'm going to her house so my dad'll let me go. But I don't go there, I'm actually with these other friends who, like me, just lie to their parents. Last

Saturday I told my mother I was going to my friend's and we went to the Wag Club. They're really choosy there and they stopped us. I thought: Oh my God, clubs are meant for eighteen-year olds. But no one suspects I'm only fifteen and they let us in. It was really nice. At 3.30 we walked round Leicester Square. I was quite scared actually. All parents say, "Oh, you can get mugged at that time in the morning," but we met these guys and they were really friendly. We couldn't go back home because it was so late. We found these places where it's open all night. We went for a meal and left about five o'clock, back to Leicester Square, chatted to some people, and wasted time so we didn't get bored, then about eleven o'clock we went back home, and arrived about twelve. It was the first time I ever spent the whole night out. I would have done it again, but my friend's parents were on holiday so we went back to her house last time.

My parents never ring up to check on me. I feel quite guilty lying to them. They really trust me so much, and here's me saying, "I'm going to sleep at my friend's house." But that tiny fear: what if something does happen to me? What am I going to tell my mum? I think it's worth it, though. I know it sounds childish but I really enjoy going out and there's no way I can tell my mum, so I have to lie to her. I hope she will never find out. I don't go out that often, and if I do go to see a film or anything I usually have to be in by eleven or twelve, or I just go to a café or a pub with a friend. The whole reason is to meet people; I'm really boy-crazy, so are all my friends.

I haven't had a boyfriend but I really want one, although I'm a bit scared. If my mum and dad found out I'd been clubbing they'd think a boy was involved, so they would probably stop me from ever going out again. They think if I have a boyfriend I'll jump into bed with him. But I won't, I just want someone to talk to. I said to Mum, do you think I can have a boyfriend, and she said when you're seventeen or eighteen – another three years! I really envy English girls sometimes, they can go out without having an excuse, they can have boyfriends, and here's me, always having to wait. I think that's how my mum was brought up. She didn't tell me about the facts of life. When I first started my periods I was eleven and I didn't know what it was. I thought I'd got a serious disease.

My mum is quite religious, we don't have to do everything but she goes to Chinese festivals and worships the gods and whatever.

They're Buddhists. I don't really understand it. They don't force me to their religion, but they feel that if you do anything wrong God will be watching you and will punish you and send you to hell. Mum says, "If you sleep with a man before marriage, God won't like it. If you do anything wrong, you'll go to hell." It really scares me. She wants me to have sex after marriage, so she tries to scare me that way. But I think if someone comes at the right time I will, not because I have to lose my virginity but because I love this person. I just won't tell them. But I'm not going to wait until after I'm married. My brothers have done it, so why can't a girl? I point out to her about my decisions and I go, "Do you mind if I marry whatever nationality?" and she says, "Whatever makes you happy," but I think she would prefer me to marry a Chinese man. If we argue I threaten them that I'm going to leave when I'm sixteen. I can marry anyone I want to, but I don't really want to. We argue over really petty things, like when my dad tells me I look like a boy. We always have arguments in Chinese, but I tend to swear at them in English. I don't say really crude words, I say, "Oh, piss off!" to my dad, and he laughs. They see it as me being immature.

I haven't got many Chinese friends, only my cousins, although I used to go to a Chinese school and made a few friends there. It wasn't like English school, the class depended on how clever you were, so our age group was between ten and fifteen. I hated it, I found it really pointless and I just couldn't learn Chinese. It was Mum who wanted me to go but I said, "Look, Mum, I won't learn anything, I'll fail my exams, what's the point in wasting money?" so I stopped going there. I hardly talk Chinese apart from with my parents, that's the only way of communicating. They speak Chinese all the time. But it's quite good them not speaking English. You can say so much without them knowing. If you're on the phone talking to a friend you can talk about boys. They want to speak English because they find it a real hassle not being able to, but they're too old now to learn.

I think I'm different to other Chinese girls. Most Chinese girls wear discreet make-up, nice flat shoes, full skirts, High Street fashion. I like dressing in second-hand clothes, and shoes – my mum calls them elephant shoes! And with short black hair, big DMs, and jeans. She did object to things I wore but now they're more okay about it. I said, "Look, Mum, I'm different, you should be proud of me, not hate me." But my mum always sticks up for me. I can talk to her much better than my dad. If I've got a problem I can tell her, whereas my dad's just there, and he wouldn't know what to do anyway. I get on with my dad, but we just tease each other, he doesn't really know the real me. Sometimes, though, I really do wish to be English, and have Westernised parents, although I don't think there's that much difference.

Compared to English parents, my parents are strict, but compared to some Chinese parents, I'm really lucky. Most Chinese parents won't even let their daughter out at night-time unless they've got a brilliant excuse, whereas I can go out and I can spend the night at my friend's. I think my parents are a lot more easy-going now because they've brought up two older boys and they've been through it all before so they can handle me a bit easier. We're generally a happy family, we all get on. They really do trust me in some ways, but I want to enjoy myself. When I'm older I can be nicer to my parents and do things without having to lie. But I'm just a hypocrite! If I had a daughter and she turned out just like me I'd really hate that!

Most people really complain about being a teenager, saying it's such a drag with parents, and not being able to make any decisions, but I think it's brilliant. I'm not an adult and I'm not a child. I can rebel to my parents but they're always there to back me up and help me out. When else can you be really freaky? I don't regret the things I've done so far. I've enjoyed my life, as long as I don't mess it up completely. My parents want me to have a good education, my mum doesn't expect me to get A's but she expects me to try. My dad thinks I'm kind of dumb, and that's why I want to get good grades. When I go back for the fifth year I'll really study – no more clubbing for me! I think I should pull my socks up a bit, not lie to my mum so much, then I'll be okay. I feel really happy at the moment, but I feel confused as well sometimes. I reckon when I've passed through my teenage life I won't want it over again. I couldn't handle all this pressure.'

ANNA

Having a younger brother can cause a lot of aggravation! Eighteen-year-old Anna is at school taking A levels, unlike her brother Tom, who left school at sixteen and is employed

7

and doing a YTS course. She complains bitterly that he and she are treated quite differently, even though he is two years younger. Both Anna and her brother are a year behind at school because a few years ago the family left their home in the north-west of England to spend three years in South Africa, where her father had taken a contract job. He now works as production manager in a small firm, while her mother works full-time as a library assistant. Anna gets a monthly clothes allowance and also has a Saturday job. She's very much looking forward to leaving home and going to a polytechnic next year.

'Tom and I have never really got on well. When we were both at school we were supposed to take the washing-up in turns and that worked okay apart from a few arguments at the weekend. But now when I say, "It's not fair, I have to do the dishes and he doesn't," Mum says, "That's because he's at work all day." But *I've* been at college all day, which is just as stressful as working; they seem to think it's an easy option. My boyfriend doesn't do anything round at his house either. On Sunday if he comes to tea with me I have to wash up too, but if Tom has his girlfriend round to tea he doesn't wash up, Mum lets him off everything. It's always "He's been at work, he's tired." It's petty things but when it happens all the time it makes me angry and I'll have a big row with Mum and Dad.

I'm jealous of Tom because he's allowed to do things, like he's only sixteen and he can drink as much as he wants, he has cans in his room. Whereas I couldn't go to a pub until I was seventeen and if I've been out it's "Have you been drinking, how much have you had to drink?" I say, "You treat him differently to how you treat me," and they say, "Well, you're a girl." I hate that. I say, "But I'm eighteen," and they say, "You should be responsible and mature, then, shouldn't you?" Anything I say just causes problems and arguments. I passed my driving test a month ago and every time I want to borrow the car there's an inquisition. Tom's getting driving lessons for his birthday and I bet that even if he doesn't get a car of his own he'll be able to use our car and I won't be able to use it.

It's the same with homework. Tom's doing a course for three years as part of his YTS, but it's me they always bug about doing homework. He'll just mess around all day, he'll phone his girlfriend and she'll come round and he won't get bugged about it at all.

Perhaps it's because he's got a job, whereas if I don't get my A levels I won't have anything. I think he's also treated differently because he's the youngest child. If I were the youngest I think I'd be able to go out if Tom was going to the same place so that he could keep an eye on me. I tell my boyfriend that it's getting on my nerves and he says, "It's different with a boy," and I tell him that's sexist. Then he goes, "Oh there she goes again!" It's not fair but that's the way it is. Parents treat boys and girls differently from when they're little. What's more, Tom doesn't get told off for coming in late. When I was his age, if I came in a few times late when I was going out with someone, I got "Be in at eleven o'clock from now on and if you're going out, you're not going with him!" When I'm out I feel guilty for not being in!

When I was doing O levels it was "Get your O levels, they're the key to your future." So I worked quite hard. But I wanted to leave and get a job. Then you can do what you like, you can go out, buy a car, have friends. But I was heavily encouraged to stay on and I was a bit cheesed off about that. In theory it's "Anna should get an education", but in practice it's "Tom is the big man". They say I should get a good job, but in reality I think they mean get a good job so that you'll be able to leave work and have your children so that you can get maternity leave for a year. They still think I'll meet some person and get a good standard of living, a two-car family and all that. So I want my A levels so that I can go away next year. I want to get out of this horrible town. I feel guilty because I'm the only one in the house that's not working. Once I leave home and just come back for holidays I think it will be better. I cause arguments because I want to make my point known. Like if I say, "When I was sixteen I couldn't do this, but Tom can," I just get "Don't be so petty and selfish, he's at work all day, don't pick on him." And I say to them if we'd stayed here and not gone abroad I'd have been at polytechnic by now and left home. My dad says if you don't like it you know what you can do, and he means move out. I say, "But I can't move out," and he says, "Exactly, so you'll have to stick it like this. And while you're living in this house you'll do as you're told." We both get treated like that, but Tom can say "I pay my way," because he pays Mum his keep.

A lot of deals go on at home. Like on Friday I wanted to borrow the car so I said I'd do the dishes. Or it's "I'll give you a lift if you dry up, or if you hoover the house." I want to go on holiday next year with my friends but I can't afford it so I asked Mum and Dad to help me out a bit. They said, "Well, you've not been revising very much lately." So if I do some revision, maybe they'll help me. But we still had a blazing row about it: "Why should we help you out, you do nothing in this house." But I do. The other night I got in from college at ten to five, brought the washing in because it was raining, put the dishes away and laid the tea. When they got in it was "Oh, you're a good girl." But I feel the things I do go unrecognised. If I've had a row with Mum and Dad over something that's bugging me I run it over in my head thinking what I'm going to say to them about it, but I never say it because I know they'll just call me a cheeky bitch or something. My feelings can't come out because they'd just stop me doing things, and the first thing would be using the car, because they know I want to use it. I have to keep quite a lot of things bottled up, but I do tell some of my friends on the bus in the morning.

I wish families would talk more about their financial situation, like we're not financially well off at all really, and this house is a hundred per cent mortgaged. It's like when they bought this new car, I know it was a bit of a struggle. I asked how much it was and they said, "It doesn't concern you." Why not? All the family should discuss things like that but they won't, and they don't tell us how much they earn. It's silly, but all our lives it's been like that. And we never talk about sex in our family, it's taboo. Mum has never sat me down and said, "These are the facts of life, Anna." I know some people whose mothers are very trendy and they can talk to them but I can't, I'd rather tell a friend.

Maybe it's stupid but my mum had a miscarriage and lost her first child and I feel I replaced it. Perhaps this is why I didn't make that bond with her or whatever it is. I don't know why we're not close. I wish I could tell her that I'm not a virgin, but she wouldn't respect me then. I don't think we'll ever talk about it. I do tell Tom things though, and I know he won't tell on me. Tom and my dad have private jokes, they have a laugh and they can swear and talk about sex in a funny way, not in a serious way.

I think my family would be happier if they let us be our own person, not what *they* want us to be. Parents want to bring you up how they weren't brought up, they want you to be better. Even if you rebel against it they say, "It's only because we're doing the best for you." You end up being responsible for their hopes for you and then you feel you're letting them down. I know they want me to do well and that they're thinking of my interests. They want us to be middle-class. Like with education, working-class parents would say leave and get a job, but middle-class parents say, "You should get A levels and get a good job." They've tried to bring us up in the middle-class type of culture so we'll do that to our kids. I say to them, "Who do you think you are?" I'm horrible for saying it, but they were brought up working-class and my mum and her sister lived in a council house.

Although Dad and Mum both went to grammar school, and Mum wanted to be a teacher, when it came to sixteen they couldn't afford to go to college, they had to get a job and leave. Perhaps that's got something to do with it. I think they try to be snobs. They said to me, "You can be something lower than you are, but we've got our values." My grandad said, "You're not going into *more* education?" He thinks I should get a secretarial job but I don't want that. I want a really good job, and to travel abroad. The only way I can get away from here next year is to do well at school now. The other day Tom said, "You're lucky because you'll be able to leave." And I said, "But you're lucky, Tom, because you've got money now and I haven't."'

DENISE

Denise was born long after her three brothers. She is fifteen and they are thirty-one, twenty-nine and twenty-six, and the eldest has left home and married. Her mother says she always wanted a girl but they had to wait until they could afford it. She gets on well with her elder brothers but not with the younger one; they have terrible rows. Her mother has never worked since getting married to her father, who is the director of a small company. Denise comes into conflict with them, particularly her father, when it comes to going out. Living some way away from the nearest town and social life means she's dependent on other people's transport, which is a constant problem. She works in a chemist's shop after school every day, and plans to leave school and get a job in a bank, which she hopes will bring the independence she yearns for.

'I don't go out very much, there's nowhere to go really without going a long way and that's a big hassle, there's only the Youth Centre. I'm normally allowed out until ten, it depends, I haven't really got a fixed time. If I arrange something without telling them, then we have a row about it. They hear so many things, they're frightened of anything happening to me. I can understand it but sometimes I think: if kids younger than me can do that, why can't I? But we've had quite a few arguments, like when I went to the Palais. First of all I wasn't going to be allowed to go, and it was only because my friend's parents said she could go that I went. But at first they said I couldn't go and I got very upset about it. I'm not allowed to do anything unless my dad says. My mum won't say, "Yes, you can go," unless I've asked my dad.

I feel like they're wrapping me up in cotton wool. I think they've got to let me find out things for myself. I tell them this and they say, "Oh, you're not as old as you think you are" – that's always the way it comes out. Obviously they've got to have some rules, but I think sometimes they go over the top. They say, "You can't go there, that's a bad place." But I don't like lying. I don't like to say I'm going to so-and-so and then go somewhere else. I would be bound to get caught and then I'd never be allowed to go anywhere, so I can't really do it. So how am I to go to a party! It can be really frustrating. People think you're really babyish because you're not allowed to. It's like eighteen is the magic age for my parents.

Mum and Dad don't like running me about, but they don't like me getting public transport. The buses only run every hour and I can't afford taxis. Luckily my brothers will run me about sometimes. There's usually a group of us go so we swap parents to take us. But I always feel guilty asking for a lift. I won't say Dad never gives me a lift, he's not an ogre, he means well at heart. They think I'm being unreasonable and I think they're being unreasonable. They've never said, "You can't wear that" or "You're not using that make-up", it's really just about going out. My friends have got the same problems. My brothers could do what they liked. I know they're boys but it's not as if I'm not careful. I wouldn't go to any areas where I thought there was going to be any trouble. I'm not that type of person.

If I could afford to move out at sixteen, I would. I don't mean it in a horrible way, but you get to the stage where they make you . . . not hate them . . . but you try to go against them because you feel it's not right them telling you what to do. It's a shame, I mean they've never hurt me, there's been no divorce, and they've never deprived me of anything, so in that way I'm lucky. But I feel they don't trust me. If I said that they'd say, "It's not you we don't trust, it's the others." Like last weekend when we went away to a holiday camp my dad's saying to me, "You know what these boys are like, they're only after one thing." But not all boys are out to rape you. I'm not stupid and I wouldn't go off with anyone I didn't trust. I don't go on my own, not on the first date anyway.

It can be awful bringing boys home. I've been quite lucky because most of the boyfriends I've had, my mum and dad have known before. I met someone last weekend, actually, and I was going to ask him to come over next week. But he's got two earrings and my dad doesn't really like boys with earrings, so it'll be embarrassing. They go very much by appearance. I like going out with older boys, but if I say, "I can't go so-and-so because of my mum and dad," they'll soon get fed up with me. I start wishing my life away because I want to get older and do what I like.

When I was younger I used to have a really close relationship with my dad. I was always his little girl and I don't think he wants to lose that. I adored him then and when I was on holiday we always used to go to the zoo together, and on a Sunday night he used to go to bed and I used to curl up with him before I went to bed and we both used to sit there reading. We do still get on, but there are times when I boil up and it all comes out. It was as soon as I got into senior school that everything changed and I started to grow up. I almost feel that my dad's turning me against him. It's not that I don't care about him, I do, I think a lot of him, and I respect that he's trying to bring me up right. But there are times when I really hate him. He kept having a go at me the other day, and when he went out – my brother had just had an argument with him as well – we were going: "Oh, we'd be better off without him. I wish he'd leave," which I know is a horrible thing to say, but you get so angry you say all things you don't mean. Sometimes I'll even say it to his face and I know I don't mean it, but I get *so* worked up that I start thinking I mean it. Sometimes I think I'm going to do something to prove to them, to make them sorry. I know all teenagers say that, but it's how you get. You feel you've got to do something to rebel against them. The more they tell you not to do something, the more you do it. Then I feel, no, I don't want to hurt myself for them. I always try and think about it before I go and do anything

I try to be open but there's lots of things I'd never discuss with my mum and dad, like a relationship I was having with a boy, I go to my friends for that. My mum and I are fairly close and she'd like me to go to her, but I get the feeling she doesn't really understand. She's got old-fashioned ways. I learned about the facts of life through school and books really. Mum and Dad never told me anything. Mum explained about periods but she didn't say anything about sex. If I wanted to go on the Pill or anything like that she wouldn't agree. I remember her saying, "Keep yourself pure before you're married," which I don't agree with at all. So I don't think I could go to her about that sort of thing. Dad never ever mentions sex. I think he thinks I'm his pure innocent daughter and I'm not going to do anything.

I haven't really had any serious relationship anyway, but I think it can come up fairly soon. I'll be sixteen then so I can go to the doctors quite openly, without them knowing. It's not something I want to do behind their backs, but I think I'll have to. I think they'd have a low opinion of me, especially my dad. I wouldn't want them to think that. Yet my dad has always said, "If you're ever in any trouble, you've got to come to us." I said, "You mean if I was pregnant you wouldn't throw me out?" He said, "No, I might blow my top, but I'd calm down and we'd sort you out and help you. If you can't come to your family with problems then who else can you turn to?"

Basically they are good parents. It's only me not being allowed to go out that we have rows about. That's the main aspect in everything. Parents are right to worry, but I think they should go about it a different way. Like organise transport in a different way, or go in a bigger group. I don't think it should mean you can't go out or can't go to places you want to.

I often worry about them because they're older. They're both fifty-five. They could live to a hundred but you hear so many people that die sooner and I think that's quite frightening. And I think perhaps if they were younger they'd understand me more. But then I know several people whose parents are quite a lot younger than mine and they still do the same things. It just seems to depend on the person. I try to look at it from my parents' point of view and I can see it, but it seems to me they can never see it from mine.

2

Fathers
and Daughters

Meeting boys in secret: Nicola
Dieting to resist: Claire
Strictly in your place: Destine

Once upon a time the stern Victorian father stood apart from his
family as a symbol of power and authority. Nowadays this is rarely
true, as fathers have generally become much more involved in
bringing up children. But they often treat sons and daughters quite
differently, and expect different things from them. Some girls
described how well they got on with their fathers, although they
probably wouldn't talk to them about personal things, as they might
their mothers. Some of them had enjoyed very close relationships
with fathers when they were small, but were having problems as
they tried to become more independent. 'He just wants to keep me
as his little girl' was a common complaint, as girls pleaded to stay
out later or go out with boys. Their fathers wanted to protect their
innocence and this makes them very cross, like Denise (in Chapter
1). You may be lucky when it comes to negotiating about boyfriends,
but if not, you may have already discovered that this can cause a lot
of hassles. Emotions can get very intense, especially if you're in
love, and then the battles commence. Here, Nicola describes the
conflict with her father over her first proper boyfriend and how she
reacted, and elsewhere (in Chapter 5) Ellie experienced her father's
anger when she not only went out with a boy he didn't like, but
was found to be having a sexual relationship.

Sex is a potential minefield. It's everywhere in magazines and on
television, but it hasn't yet become an easy subject to discuss with
parents. Even those who have a good relationship with their mother

often draw the line here. You'd think that since their parents had grown up during the 'swinging sixties', with their emphasis on sexual freedom, all this might have changed, but apparently not. As Louise says: 'I think they're embarrassed. They're always telling me how mature I am and yet matureness is being able to talk about sex freely without giggling or smiling in a stupid way. They've never once told me the facts of life. I've learnt everything I know about sex, contraception, periods, etc., from school and friends. This makes me so angry.' Out of all the girls who wrote to me, as well as those I talked to, only a few could talk freely about sex with their parents, and this was usually with mothers, rarely with fathers. Not only is it embarrassing to be talking to men about sex or contraception, but fathers' views on boyfriends and sex can be strongly disapproving: 'He's quite possessive. A lot of the time he teases me about boys, but other times he gets quite nasty and slams the phone down on them when they ring me . . . I think he'd go crazy if I dared mention sex to him. It's a closed subject.'

Some fathers find the idea of their daughter having sex quite threatening. She's no longer their innocent little girl, and they cannot easily accept this. If she gets pregnant, their reaction is even more marked. While most mothers are initially upset at such news, they soon become very supportive, while fathers often react more strongly and take longer to come to terms with it, especially if sex and contraception have never been discussed at all. Not all fathers are like this – there are some who are very open-minded about these issues, and about sexuality in general. Maria, for instance (in Chapter 9), was surprised and relieved that her father reacted in a reasonable way when he discovered she was having a lesbian relationship.

The amount of freedom and independence you get – whether you can have boyfriends, or sex before marriage – can be greatly affected by what sort of religious or cultural background you come from. Even in Patricia's family (in Chapter 5), which is very liberal about freedom and boyfriends, sex before marriage is taboo because of her parents' Irish Catholic background. Others have far more restricted lives. For instance, girls and women from Asian families, like Pardeep (in Chapter 9), find their freedom closely monitored. Men are very dominant in Muslim cultures, but the pattern of life for women in such families established in Britain can vary a lot and also depends on whether they pursue education or marry outside

16

their culture. Destine, from a Turkish Cypriot family, describes her own experiences and her relationship with her father. It's particularly hard for girls like Pardeep and Destine to resist, because if a girl's reputation is put in doubt, this can have adverse consequences for both her and her family. Rebellion can be tricky in any family, and people go about it in various ways. Some have stormy arguments for the right to do what they want; some say little but sneak off and do it anyway; while others find different ways to resist. For example, Claire's reaction to her strict father was expressed in losing weight to show that she could control her own life.

NICOLA

Nicola has two brothers and a sister who are much older than her: she is seventeen and they're in their late twenties and thirties. Her brothers have left home, and she and her sister live with their parents in the West Midlands. Her father works as a financial adviser, and her mother does baby-minding. As the youngest and a girl, she feels overprotected, especially in relation to boys. When, about eighteen months ago, she started going out with her first real boyfriend, her father was very disapproving. There were angry scenes and the relationship was banned, something that Nicola just couldn't accept. Over the next few months, trust within the family reached a low ebb. Now, after a year and a few other confrontations, things have improved and she is even planning a holiday with her current boyfriend. She is taking a BTEC course in information technology and computer studies and sometimes works for her brother, a computer analyst, which gives her a bit of money and independence.

'I'd been going out with Andy for about three months when it first happened with my dad. He just got completely the wrong idea about what was going on. It was because Andy was twenty, Dad said, "He only wants one thing off you," but I knew he didn't because I knew what he was like. I'd known him from about three years before. I think Dad just didn't want his little girl to be touched. She had to be pure. Andy was playing cricket at the cricket club and I was scoring in the same match. My brother forgot to get me a lift home with one of the other players so Andy took me. Afterwards we went out and I got home about nine o'clock. I wasn't strictly meant to be home for seven, but it was expected of me because all the other players were coming back. My dad was watching and he absolutely aimed for Andy. I just ran into the house and locked myself in the bedroom. I could see Dad was shaking Andy and I was thinking: oh God, don't hit him please. Andy was shouting. I was thinking: What the hell is going on? Why is he doing this? I couldn't understand it. Then we had sessions in Dad's study, me and Dad. I was banned from seeing Andy, or if I saw him I wasn't to speak to him. I had to ignore him completely. But I didn't.

After Dad had a scene with Andy I felt like killing him, and when he told me I couldn't go out with him I felt very alienated. Over at the club, where I met Andy, my dad's on the committee and they all took his side. It was like "It's his little girl." Which is true, because I'm the youngest and he's more cautious with me. He didn't really catch us doing anything – Andy had his arm round me, or we were holding hands – but Dad just went completely over the top. He was my first proper boyfriend, and Dad just didn't understand that.

My mum knew I still saw Andy but she didn't tell my dad. I'd started back to school then and Andy picked me up from school every day. He'd drop me off home by the traffic island and say, "I'll meet you at the park," then I'd be out for two hours. Mum would know where I'd been because I'd come back with a smile on my face. I'd be happy for a change. She knew when I didn't see him because I was really miserable, really niggly. Dad didn't find out, in spite of the silly excuses I made. One half-term week I made up that I was going to my friend's every day and I went to Andy's for nine o'clock in the morning and I left there at six every night. We'd go out for the day or something. It was great. I was thinking: "Hah, Dad! I'm not doing what you told me to do." I thought: who cares! I was just sixteen and Andy was twenty. On my birthday Andy took me out. My dad was away and my mum was at work, and Andy parked his car in our drive. My brother is a copper and he passed in a police car and took the registration number, looked it up and it was Andy's mother's. So of course my brother confronted me at the dinner table and I just ran upstairs. My sister-in-law followed me, she was trying to imply that he'd raped me. I was crying my eyes out wondering what the hell she was going on about. She was saying, "Do you want me to go and tell Andy it's all over?" I said, "It's not over." But as far as my dad was concerned it was.

I thought: I don't care, if they chuck me out I'll go and move in with Andy. Nobody seemed to have any sympathy for me. We weren't even doing anything then, although we did sleep together eventually. God knows how he convinced me into it because I didn't want to. I thought: I'll sleep with someone when I love them, that'll be all right. I did it more for him than for me, because I knew how much he loved me. I slept with him three times, then I finished with him. I don't know what happened. I just got really angry with him on the phone. I wanted some time to myself, but I didn't say that, it all came out completely different. I'd just had enough. I was continually being questioned by Mum and Dad, asking me what I was doing. It was "What time are you going to be in by? If you're not in, then you're not going out again." So I finished with him; I could hear how upset he was. Then I phoned him up the next day but he wasn't there, his mum said he'd gone back to university. I would have said, "I want to go back with you desperately." But I couldn't phone him there so I just left it. I wrote him about four letters but I didn't post them.

When I was going out with Andy, my parents didn't trust me. I think my dad was frightened Andy was going to try and take advantage of me. Mum trusted me but it depended what mood she was in. Sometimes it would be question time: "Where are you going? Who are you going with?" Then she'd phone up the people and say, "Is Nicola going out with Annette today?" All my friends would cover up for me, they knew how much I wanted to see him. At the time I didn't know if Andy was worth it or not. I was pushing my parents to see how far I could go, but I didn't realise I was going over the top with it. I should have stopped seeing him but I didn't want to.

Last year my dad seemed to get worse and worse and I just gave up with him. I didn't bother to speak to him. I used to be angry at everything, but now I'm a lot calmer and free and easy. I've changed in the last six months. Anything that he says to me now – like he goes on about me smoking at the moment – I just turn off and think he's only doing it because he loves me. It's all right at the moment, I've regained his trust again. We went through a stage

19

when I'd have to be in at nine o'clock, and I'd be back on time. I got his trust for doing that. I thought: sod it, if I have to be back by then it doesn't bother me. I'll go out and make use of the time I've got. Now anywhere, if I've said I'm going to be in by eleven, and if it gets to a quarter to eleven and I'm going to be a bit late I'll phone them. Before, I just left it. I'd get in at quarter past twelve and Dad got absolutely angry. Now I consider what they're going to feel.

I'd say to anyone else: if you value your parents, it's best to stick at it. Most of the time I found it best to cut myself off from them, but I've got back into the situation where they trust me again. It took a year to regain their trust, but I've done it. I now look back and think: Why did I lose their trust? Was it my fault? I think it was half my fault and half my dad's fault. Him not trusting me in the first place and me just rebelling. But if I hadn't rebelled against that, I probably would have done it against something else. It was like Dad was enforcing the power he had over me. But he didn't have any, because all I did was rebel against him and we grew further apart. Now we're just about back to normal. He knows I'll tell the truth and he can rely on me. But sometimes I feel that my parents treat me like an adult and other times as a child. The other week Dad said to me, "You're seventeen now, you're an adult." But he still sees me as a little girl. Mum's changed her attitude towards me over the last few months. She treats me more as a woman.

I do love my parents, but most of the time it's still difficult. At one point recently I moved out and went to live with my brother for two weeks; my parents were being really difficult. After I'd been away for about five days my mum rang up and said, "Oh I do miss you, Nicola." And I thought: oh God, that means I've got to go back. But I stuck it out for another week. It was great at my brother's and his new girlfriend was there. But then again it was nice to be home, because I'd missed Mum shouting at me, and Dad warbling on about absolutely nothing, telling me how good my life is. There's the odd moment, like when I got back after moving out, I just sat down at the dinner table and my mum put her arm round me and I've never felt so good in my life. And there's times when my dad will come up to me and say something like, "I'm glad you're here." It's only now and then, but it makes me feel as though I'm really wanted. Other times they say, "When the hell are you going to move out?" They actually allowed me this year to go on holiday with my friends. I've also started going out with someone else now, but it's been ages. I haven't been able to cope with anyone else. I've been through a bad time – I mean they could have chucked me out, my dad kept saying that he would, but when it came to the crunch I know he never would really, because I'm the baby.'

CLAIRE

Claire is full of energy for her first year at university, where she's just started a degree in biology. Although her parents were not very well off, they were very keen on education and sent her to a private school. Here she found herself under a lot of pressure to do well and take lots of exams. She got thirteen O levels and three A levels. Although the family were quite close, she was always a bit afraid of her father, a fitness enthusiast who often teased her about her weight. Three years ago, when she was fifteen, she started cutting down on food and also took up sport and fitness training herself. It was some time before her parents realised how thin she was getting.

'I was in my O-level year when it started. It had been building up for a long time because when I was younger, my family life was very intense. My father's all right really, he's just got a rather volatile temper. You can't speak to him in that mood, he'll just explode at you. It caused a lot of misery when we were younger, and I was so scared of him that I wouldn't say anything when he came into the house, then I'd start talking and being normal as soon as he went out. If we were on a car journey we weren't allowed to talk or giggle or anything, or he'd turn round and say, "You! Shut up!" I think that's why I was so quiet and shy and lacked confidence with people at school, because I expected them to explode like my dad.

I'd always been well developed for my age and I started my periods when I was about ten. I went to a mixed junior school, mostly boys, and the boys were going "She's getting big. She's growing breasts", and all that. They teased me and I used to go around hiding it. Then my dad would say, "You're too fat," and make all these cutting comments about it. Perhaps he was just teasing me, but I took it rather personally. My dad used to have a weight problem when he was younger, and looked old for his age because he was going bald. He got very upset about it and became a total fitness fanatic, but he went a bit over the top. He went on one of those diets with special drinks. He looked nice and friendly when he was chubby, but he went all gaunt and skinny-looking. He's not like that any more, he's relaxed a bit now.

I think getting anorexic was mostly rebelling against him. Most of my eating problems came from my dad being like that himself. When he was being the real fitness freak, we all felt he was getting really cold and self-obsessed, and he used to get into tempers all the time. I think the actual springboard where it all took off was one day we went to play tennis. I hadn't eaten anything for about a week, but I hadn't actually lost very much weight because I'd only just started not eating. Towards the end of the game I said, "Golly, I'm really hungry," and he looked at me and said, "You're not exactly underweight, are you?" And I was so upset about that. I wasn't overweight, I was normal. Just because I happened to say I was hungry! Obviously it had been building up, but that was the match that sparked it off. Subconsciously I thought: I'll show him; and if he stopped eating a certain thing, I'd give it up as well, to show I was on an equal level – I didn't need milk in tea, I didn't need butter. Everything he did, *I* did to an extreme. He did get into a few tempers with me for not eating. Then he realised it was because he'd been like it himself. He'd say to me, "You're miles too thin, look at the way your stomach goes in," and I'd say, "You can talk, look at you."

I never thought: "I'm on a diet," I just cut down until I was on a bit of fruit and a small main meal. I was eating the absolute minimum. I never caused upsets about eating with the family, but I'd pretend I was really full. It was "You're getting very thin, you've got to do something about it." I got very upset about that because I thought: I can eat what I want to, why are they trying to pressurise me? My mum got cross when she cooked things and I wouldn't eat very much, but she was quite good really. I didn't talk to them very much about it. It was an unspoken thing, an atmosphere we had, and it wasn't very nice. There seemed to be this tenseness every time a meal came up.

I managed to lose a pound or two a week. I considered self-induced vomiting, but I tried it once and it didn't work. I thought:

this is disgusting, I can't do this. I also had a stage when I'd go into the kitchen and get all these jars out and take a little bit out of each one. I'd probably eat a handful of food and I'd feel I'd eaten a whole houseful. I used to take laxatives to get rid of it because I wasn't used to eating that much. Every little thing felt like loads and loads. I'd feel really sick and sit next to the toilet all night. My periods stopped six months before I was really losing weight, which was rather odd. I went to the doctor and said I'd been doing a lot of training recently, and she said that's probably the reason, and I should put weight back on gradually and they'll start again. I put a bit on and they still hadn't started and we went for a lot of X-rays and examinations. They did eventually start just after my eighteenth birthday, which I was dead pleased about. It's all right to stop for six months, but not a couple of years.

At that age I wanted to be more independent and they weren't letting me and I didn't know how to express what I felt. But I loved being hungry because I was in control of my own body, it felt great. I'd read about anorexia and thought: no, that can't be me; but I realised it was and I knew why girls go like this, what they were feeling inside. It's just wanting to control something for yourself when you can't. With me it was having very strict parents. Unfortunately it has the opposite effect because it makes parents more protective. They're always making sure you eat up and asking you about your private habits. I had to lie to them quite a lot, which made it worse.

The worst time was on holiday that year. I'd got this little bikini on and they were saying, "You can eat more than that, you're like a starving bird." I said, "It's up to me, isn't it?" and we had this massive row. Mum looked at my ribs and said, "That's disgusting". I felt: so what? Other people are thin and they don't get into trouble about it. Dad brought the scales out and I was about six stone three pounds. I just said, "Golly, I didn't realise I was that light." Although I did. But I felt really bad about it and thought I'd try to eat whatever they gave me. For the next half year, every couple of weeks they asked me how much I weighed and I think when they saw me recovering they realised I was more mature than they thought, and I was quite pleased about that. I think my dad felt a bit guilty that he'd often criticised me for being quite chubby when I was younger. Then I met my first boyfriend, and that changed my whole life. It was like there was a purpose to it and I wasn't worried about eating any more.

I was very lucky it didn't really destroy my family life. I realised what was happening. If I'd actually stopped eating rather than just cutting down, then it would have done. I just caused a bit of friction, got a bit of attention for a while. You've got to pick yourself up before it takes control of you. It's an obsession. I became very different from what I was like before. I got a bit distant from my parents, more introverted. I was thinking about myself more than other things around me. I'd look at weight charts and I'd see the bottom of the scale was seven stone, so I set the target there, that was the most I'm ever going to weigh. And then it would be like six stone and a quarter. I got self-absorbed, I was studying for O levels, and I had this obsession of writing things out really neatly, and being really organised. It became a ritual to get up at half-past six every morning; do a certain number of press-ups; a certain number of exercises; have so many branflakes; walk so many miles to school. Now I'm dead scruffy, terribly disorganised. That's the most different thing about me. I do whatever happens at the time. It doesn't bother me if I get out of routine because I don't have a routine any more. It's wonderful!

Looking back, I'd ask any other girls who felt like me to think what it's going to do to their family. Can you use your self-control more constructively and try to find a better way to make your feelings known? Perhaps people who develop anorexia are afraid to grow up, because your chest gets flatter and your hips get narrower, you're like a child. I was the opposite, though, because I did want to grow up. I wanted my independence. There's various reasons, and there's a horrible attitude, too, that you just want to diet and look slim. But you don't put yourself through all that pain just because of that. I know a lot of models in magazines are really skinny, but you don't do it just to look like a model. That attitude really annoys me. People who say that are totally wrong. I didn't really feel better about my body. If I looked in the mirror I couldn't see any difference. Being in control was the main thing for me. But I prefer myself now to what I was then. All my ribs stuck out and I was bony and hard. In a way it was quite satisfying because I felt I'd mastered myself, but I think it's more attractive not to be like a rake! After I recovered I began to get much more independent and self-confident. I built myself up to feel: I'm a normal girl and I've got nothing to be ashamed of. I'm quite proud of myself – in fact I've got quite a big ego now!

It's brilliant here at university. Originally I thought it would be all boring swots, but it's really good. My parents used to have this image of me as being very quiet, conscientious, and very hard-working, and I didn't feel like that. I don't have any strong ambitions. I think you do your work to get it over and done with and then go out and enjoy yourself. Now they see me drinking and talking with my boyfriends, and I've established that I'm not quite like they thought I was. When they came to visit, I expected them to be really intrusive and ask me if I was eating properly, but my mum said, "You seem to be managing all right, I'm glad you're enjoying it so much." They say, "Just do whatever you can"; they seem to accept that I'm living my own life. They're not being possessive any more. I'm really pleased about it, and we get on much better now.'

Most people have heard of *anorexia nervosa* these days, and it's said that one in every two hundred girls aged sixteen to eighteen will suffer from it to some extent. Its severity may vary a lot, but it usually involves strict dieting, exercise, and sometimes excessive use of laxatives to get rid of food. A related and more serious condition called *bulimia* involves self-induced vomiting. Girls often stop having periods for a while. Obviously putting the body through such extremes can be quite harmful, and can have serious and even fatal consequences if continued over a long period of time. There are links between anorexia and what's going on within the family, as Claire's experience shows. If you're concerned that this is happening to you (or any of your friends), you really need to seek professional help. (See Contacts section at the end of this book.)

DESTINE

Destine's family are Turkish Cypriot, from Northern Cyprus, where many of the family still live. Her mother came to London when she was twelve, and her dad when he was eighteen. Destine, almost eighteen, is the third eldest of six sisters, who range in age from twenty down to six, and she has a baby brother of two-and-a-half. Her eldest sister is in a rather unsatisfactory marriage, and the second eldest is babysitting at home. Destine is taking A levels in art, textiles and Turkish, and some GCSEs. Her closest relationship is with her seventeen-year-old sister, who is doing a YTS course in hairdressing. The two younger sisters are at school. In a traditional Turkish family, girls' lives are very restricted, and Destine's is no exception.

'My dad was much stricter with my eldest sister. We have arranged marriages, and they got her engaged when she was sixteen. She wasn't too sure, but she and the boy talked to each other and afterwards she said yes. He was about twenty-five. We had the engagement in a big hall, but she split up with him that night when they got home. He was from Cyprus and they've got different ways of doing things, they're old-fashioned. But I think she was just too young. We also have something called "soz", which is before you get engaged; it's like "I promise to give my daughter to you." There's no word for it in English. My sister got "soz" to another boy six months later, but it didn't work out again. Then about a year ago she met the boy she's married to. I can't really say it's working out, and that's why it's scary with boys who don't come from here. He comes from Turkey and it's not that we don't get on with them, but we're different.

The Turkish people in Turkey call us Greeks because we've been brought up with Greeks, and the Cyprus side don't like it either. My dad and him don't really like each other, but my sister said she wanted him. They all say he only married for the passport and he's not treating her very well, because when he gets his wages he sends them back to feed his family in Turkey. Then he and my sister started having rows, and she said, "I'm not sleeping with you unless you get me my settee next week!" So he got that, and then she did it for the TV. But he should buy all that anyway. He knows we don't really like him because he doesn't look after her. I want my sister to get divorced but she's got no confidence in herself. She believes in our father's traditions. He says even if your husband is bad, just stay with him for your own sake so that people won't talk about you. I don't believe in that. I tell her, "Don't care about what other people say, just think of yourself."

My sister left school when she was fifteen and stayed at home, smoking and watching TV all day, so they wanted to get her married. It's mainly my nan who drove her to get married, and she started nagging about me six months ago. My dad turned round and said, "She's doing her A levels and GCSEs", and she said, "Oh, forget about that. When she gets a husband she's going to sit at home, clean up, cook, have babies." But my dad shut her up and I haven't seen her for ages. They like you to be married at seventeen or eighteen, but they've learnt over the years, and they don't want us to be like my sister, they feel guilty for that. That's why they're trying to be a bit more modern with the rest of us. My second sister says she doesn't want to get married at all, because we all see our sister in her situation and it puts us totally off men, let alone marriage! I don't want to get married until I'm in my thirties. If I was working they'd try to get me married at about twenty, but they respect what I'm doing, and I'm going to be studying until I'm about twenty-three. My dad wants me to be a fashion designer, as this is his family background. I wouldn't be able to do that if I got married.

Turkish men, like my sister's husband, won't let their wives go out and work. Some of them are quite modern, but she's unlucky. She got engaged to one, she got soz to one, she's got married to this one, and all three were like that. They just want you to stay at home and clean up, and make the food when they come home. My dad's like that too. Mum works at home as a machinist and she wanted to go out and work the other day and he said, "No, I want you to stay at home." My mum's the type who laughs a lot and mucks about and he doesn't like her going out, he prefers her to be at home because he's suspicious-minded. He doesn't want anyone to talk. There's quite a few Turks in this country and rumours get round to them very quickly. It's like being in a village in Cyprus. They all meet up in the Turkish cafés and start saying, "Thingy's daughter's done this and that." And my dad always goes in them and he says to us, "The worst thing I could hear is them talking about my daughter in the café. I would hate that. I would hang myself and hang my daughter for it!" For boys it's different. My dad actually flinged about at a young age and he got many women pregnant. He's made loads of mistakes, but he doesn't think about things like that. He's the type you've got to look up to all the time.

My father won't allow us to go out with boys although the majority of Turkish girls nowadays sneak out. But my mum has been brought up more modern, she's sneaked us out to a disco one or two times, without my dad knowing. He'll let us out but my friends have to come round to be looked over and he prefers girls who have got the same background as me. He wouldn't ever let me go to a disco because it's late hours, although I can go to the cinema with a girlfriend. He prefers me to go out with my sister, and I prefer it too, I feel more secure. We've only got a year between us. I trust her, we're like best friends, and it doesn't come like that for everyone. You can always break up with a friend but I don't think you can break up with a sister, even though we have fights. I always tell my sister whatever happens and she tells me too.

Even though my mum's quite soft I can't tell her everything, and I can't talk to my dad at all. He's brought us up so shy of him. When he used to bring up the subject of marriage, I used to go really red. He never talks about boys, and only now we're learning gradually to talk about marriage in front of him. We only talk about what happens at school or at work, or about films and things. Some meals we eat together, but sometimes we take our meals up to our bedrooms, or we sit in the front room, talking to each other. If I've got something to tell my sister privately I'll say, "Shall we go to our bedrooms and do some homework?" otherwise they get suspicious, they're so dirty-minded. When my dad comes to see what I'm doing, he looks round at my lipsticks and things. He doesn't mind make-up, but there's loads of other things that he tells me I'm too young for. My mum and dad don't approve of me wearing trousers but they don't mind miniskirts because my mum usually gets them from my uncle's factory and he likes to see them on us. But I'd never wear a swimming costume in front of my dad. He'd let me but I'm too shy. If it was on a roof with a lot of workmen with me in my little bikini, all right, but not my dad, not even with a swimming costume on, never mind a bikini! I just feel very uncomfortable, I feel dirty too. That's why I don't want to go on holiday with my dad. When I went with just my mum I was free and I really enjoyed it.

We were always brought up to know that sex before marriage wasn't acceptable, and so I thought someone was a tart to go with anyone. Sometimes I think if you feel strongly for a boy it's all right, but I don't believe in sex before marriage myself, I'd still prefer to wear my white dress. I don't always agree with my parents but I respect their traditions, so I wouldn't rebel. I'm more into my education. It's not worth doing it just for the experience. Most of my English friends look so depressed and bored. I think it's because they've got so much freedom. They've gone out with boys and slept with them at the age of fifteen and they're not very happy. Everyone's got a problem; if it's not sex it's something else. I think I'm lucky. I'm well off, I'm not being beaten or anything.

I haven't really had any boyfriends but I don't really mind as I'm still at school. I did have a crush on someone when I was fifteen for about two years, but his parents are from Turkey and his father wouldn't let him go with me because I was a Cypriot. He was all right, it was kissing and cuddling, but not outside in public. You never know who's watching, so we went in little alleys. He knows what Turkish families are like too and his father was really strict. But he's the old-fashioned type, he didn't want me to go to the sports centre with him and wear shorts as he didn't want anyone looking at my legs! I thought afterwards: we're not even going out with each other properly and he's doing this, so I can't imagine me as his poor wife! I'm glad it didn't work out.

My dad's got this thing about boys, but on other things he's all right, like about what you eat and if you don't go to the mosque. I don't really believe in it that much. I don't really like saying that because I think somebody is listening. I've never seen a Koran in my life; if anyone asks me "Are you a Muslim?", I just say yes because my parents count me as one, but I'm not. I eat beef, bacon and pork and that. I've only been to the mosque a couple of times, once just to pray and once because someone in the family died. People from Cyprus aren't as strict Muslims as in Turkey, because they're really mixed with the Greeks and the Greeks are Christians. And if anyone asks, "What are you?", I say Turkish, although I've never been to Turkey, and we've got no family there. Most of my friends are from Turkey and they speak really good Turkish. My Turkish isn't all that outstanding; there's a sort of posh Turkish, but we're the cockney ones! We talk English at home most of the time. Our parents don't like it, especially when we get visitors from Cyprus, but I think: God, we've been brought up here, it's too much!

My dad doesn't really know me. He thinks I'm the type who goes to school, doesn't look at anyone, just looks at the floor! Although I've said things about my dad I still love and respect him. In a way I love him more than I love my mum, he's really good to me

29

sometimes. He annoys me but he doesn't mean to do it. I always think about things like death and I think I'd cry more over my father than I'd cry over my mum. I think it's because he shows me more attention than my mum. He used to treat me like his son when I was little because I was tomboyish and I used to look like him so much. He's got faith in me, and he knows if I say I'm going to do something, I'll do it.'

3

Somewhere to Belong

Two families but no real home: **Rachel**
Suddenly a family: **Alex**

It's nice to feel you belong somewhere. It's good to have a place where you know you're welcome, and you can feel relaxed and be yourself. Home can be like that, and for some people their family is where they belong. For others, the family may mean something different, as some girls have found through trying to fit into new families after their parents have split up. Today's high divorce rate is matched by an increasing number of remarriages. This means a lot of children have to learn to live with a new mother or father, and maybe new brothers and sisters as well. Because mothers tend to be given custody of the children, it's more common to find yourself living with a stepfather, with occasional visits to your father's home.

Some stepfamilies are very happy and successful, and everyone enjoys being a 'complete' family again. But getting on with stepfamilies can also be fraught with difficulties, even if they're nice. If you've started to enjoy an exclusive relationship with one parent, this will be spoilt if someone new comes on the scene. It's also hard to accept a replacement for your real mother or father, as one girl said: 'I just can't think of him as my dad. My sister can never remember having a father but I don't like him to tell me what to do like he's my real father.' New brothers and sisters can also prove a mixed experience; you like some, you hate others. It can be like that for real brothers and sisters too, but you have no choice about them, whereas with stepbrothers and sisters it seems as if the parent involved has chosen to land them in your life.

It's easy to feel rather left out if your parents have created new families for themselves. You may feel that you're somehow left over from a previous era unless your parents make an effort to ensure that you know you're loved and valued. One girl who lived with her mother, stepfather and their new baby said: 'He's a normal, caring father, but sometimes I sense that I'm left out and the happy family is just Mum, Dad and the baby. I understand that because I'm not his own daughter he feels something stronger towards the baby than he does to me, so I try not to let it get to me.'

Rachel has two half-sisters by her mum's remarriage, and new brothers and sisters from her dad's girlfriend, but she doesn't live with either of these families as she's at boarding school. She describes how she feels an outsider to both. Alex, on the other hand, is still exploring every aspect of belonging to a new and extremely large family. After years of being neglected by her mother, she was finally placed with a foster family, where she has never been happier.

RACHEL

Rachel's parents divorced twelve years ago when she was two, and her mother remarried two years later. Her stepfather is an electronics engineer in the army, so they spent six years in Germany. Because her stepfather and mother were going to Hong Kong for two years she was sent to a boarding school near London when she was twelve. Her eleven-year-old half-sister is also there. They are due back in England soon, and Rachel is looking forward to seeing them and her new baby sister. Her real father lives with his girlfriend and her two children (aged twelve and nine) and Rachel doesn't like going there much. She has eighteen months to go in this school, then she'll complete her GCSEs and A levels somewhere else.

'When I'm at school I refer to my place in Hong Kong as home, because that's where my mother is; when I'm in Hong Kong I'm always saying, "At home . . ." meaning my dad's house. But I really prefer my mum's place, there's more space, I can do what I like, whereas my dad's very protective. He doesn't like me going out much, and he won't let me stay at any of my friends' houses if they've got brothers. It makes me angry because he never knew what I was doing when he only saw me every four months or so, then as soon as I came here he was acting like some kind of big dictator, telling me what to do. He writes to my mother through his girlfriend. I feel as though they're talking about me all the time, like an object, and I always think things are going to be reported back. I'll say something like "I want to do this." His girlfriend will say, "You can't," and I'll say, "I'm allowed to do it at home." She'll say, "You're not at home, you're here." And she wrote to my mother, who said, "While Rachel is in your care it's your choice." So now every time I do something she'll produce the letter to say she's got authority to say what I can and can't do. It's so annoying.

Although I address my letters to my father, it's his girlfriend who writes back. She says Dad's busy or something. She seems to do everything, but it's better than having no reply I suppose, and she does send me whatever I ask for, like loads of stamps, but she's just not on the same wavelength. When my stepdad and my mum decided to send me here she and my dad didn't agree with private education, so she complains about it all the time. It's horrible for me because she doesn't tell my mother, she says it to me, and then I don't want to hurt my mother by telling her. They're continually talking about each other and I'm in the middle.

My mum's had a baby so I've got another half-sister now. I feel a bit funny because they're like one family, and then when I go to stay with my dad they're like a family as well, so I don't fit in. I feel a bit left out, especially at my dad's. When they do something they expect me to do the same. I tell my mum and she says to tell my dad, but I don't really tell him because I don't want to hurt his feelings. I don't like asking him for anything, it makes me feel like I'm taking a liberty.

At home I call my stepdad "dad", and I call my dad by his name. I don't think he really minds. The only thing is when I'm talking to my dad about my stepdad and I say, "My dad says this . . ." But he calls my stepdad my dad as well, which is a bit weird. It's okay when you get used to it. A lot of people in the school are like that anyway – they have parents who are divorced. My friend Jill went to her dad's wedding on Friday. It's okay at Christmas time, you get lots of presents! I get on well with my mum, but I can't talk to her about really personal things because she just starts laughing. Me and my stepdad, we do get on but we're never very close and we didn't used to get on. At one point everything I did seemed to be wrong and he was always the one telling me. If my mother had told me off I don't think I'd have taken it that badly, so I was quite rude, I suppose. He told my mum she'd have to do it, so if there's a disagreement now he won't say anything, but with my sister he's the one who says it.

They know I'm not exactly brainy but they push me into trying really hard. My sister got a scholarship here, she's brainy and it gets on my nerves sometimes. Everyone seems to expect different things of me. One minute my mum will say, "Well, if that's what you want to do, then do it." Then she'll say, "I don't think you should do that." My dad doesn't pay much attention. My mum and stepdad get so worried and sometimes I just tease them, like when I saw a programme on TV about the Sisters of Calcutta and said I wanted to be one. They were taking it so seriously! But there are some things that really interest me, like I do loads of acting and I'm in the choir, and I go and visit old people in the home, and I work in the school for the deaf and blind. But they don't really value that as it's not school work. They're only really happy when I get high marks. Last year when I got a low one they got angry.

At the beginning of last year I hadn't seen my dad's girlfriend for yonks, so she was really watching what she was doing. For some reason my dad thinks I don't like people to tell me what to do. I'm not really like that, I just don't like her to do it because she's very bossy and it bugs me. I just pretend to listen to her; I don't argue with her because that's not very nice for my dad. He knows I don't like her; I think that's why he hasn't got married to her. At the moment they're buying my grandmother's house where I used to go and stay and one of the rooms has always been mine. I didn't want them to buy it but I'm the only one who seems to have disagreed. They're decorating it for the children. I don't know whether I'm having a room there yet. I don't get told very much, I have to find it out.

I haven't really got a proper room anywhere at the moment. All my bedroom belongings are in boxes at my dad's house. In Hong Kong it's an army house, you have to have pink walls, pink carpet, everything's regulation. I've got nothing there except my bed, my bedside table and my stereo. Here I'm not allowed to have anything. I've got my bed and my locker, and we're only allowed six things on the locker. We've got hardly any space, and you can't treat it as your own room. I've got clothes spread around everywhere. I'm always losing things and wondering where they are. My mum and stepdad are going to move into a house over here, then I'm having my own room and I can take everything there. I can't wait. It's going to be so different, and I won't have to go and stay with my dad all the time.

I used to think my dad was wonderful until I came here. I think it's because I see him more, and he's with his girlfriend and her children. I had him all to myself before and he used to take me out all the time. Now it's me, him and everybody else, and I feel as if I'm getting in the way sometimes. I used to think he was much better than my stepdad, but now I prefer my stepdad. My mum's hoping that when they come back to England everything will be okay. It might be, but I do feel the odd one out and they don't realise it. Nobody ever asks what I feel like or what I'm going to do. I want to do so many things, but I don't want to tell them because they'll treat it as a joke or something I'll grow out of. Mum's always saying how much she misses me, but when we're at home we argue. Sometimes we get on really well, I'll sit on the bed and tell her what I've done. She's not that old, she's always borrowing my clothes and I'm always borrowing hers. It's really nice at times – like Christmas, when we do things together – but they seem to get on so well, just them three. They're so much like a family all the time. I'm so different to them, they like meeting people and I prefer to stay in and do something by myself.

School would be really good if you could go out more. But then in boarding school you're in a kind of shell, you don't know what's going on in the outside world. We get to watch television but only at certain times. We come up from school at six, have supper till quarter to seven, then prep from 7.30 to 8.30. Then we go to bed at half-past nine. You say, "I'm going to watch TV later," but someone will come in and you'll end up sitting and talking. I haven't had many boyfriends because of being here. You can't go anywhere or do anything, and you can't have phone calls. In a way it makes you feel as if you've grown up because sometimes I go to London, but not in other ways because I can't do anything like go to parties.

I don't really get on with my sister although I kind of look after her here. If people say something to her that hurts her feelings then I'll stick up for her. We've never been that close. She comes up sometimes, usually when she wants something. When I was her age I was much more mature, she's a bit like a baby. She wants to leave this school, and if she does, I'll have a whole year here while she'll be at home. That might make it worse because they'll be in a family atmosphere all the time and I'll only be there for the odd weekend. I do get lonely and depressed at school, and sometimes at home. I don't really have anyone I can confide in. My best friend here hasn't really been my best friend for that long, and she's got family problems as well so although we talk about it we don't make a habit of it. My grandmother's quite good to talk to but I don't see her very often.

I think life will be better when my mother comes back and we're actually a family again; it's really strange having to go abroad all the time. I'd really like to be in a family where I don't have any brothers or sisters, where I can get on with what I want to do. Having two families makes me want to have something of my own and not to always feel I'm just going from one to the other.'

ALEX

Alex has a huge family. There are ten altogether, two adults and eight children (not forgetting three others who have moved out into their own flats nearby), comprising three boys and five girls ranging in age from nine to twenty. Four of them, including sixteen-year-old Alex, are being fostered. Alex is about to start going to college to do a creative arts course. She wants to be a singer, and has already won some talent shows and written some songs.

Alex was born in London; her mother came from Nigeria but she doesn't know anything about her dad, except that he's Jamaican. She has an elder sister, Joan, aged twenty-five, who has a different father. Her mother always wanted a son, and she didn't like having two daughters, so nine years ago she sent Joan to Africa to live with her father. While her mother worked as a nurse, Alex was day-fostered or went to live with her cousins, which she didn't like as they didn't treat her well. Her mother had also treated her badly since her sister left, but this got worse when she gave up nursing. She started hitting Alex for no reason, and once she split her head open with an alarm clock. She'd beat her with a broom, or bite her. Alex was covered in marks, her clothes were ripped, and people started asking questions at school. Although she didn't like having to lie, she'd just say it was nothing. She was often left on her own for days without food or money and was taken in by her next-door neighbour. When she was older, she went round to stay with her best friend instead.

Alex could never understand why her mother was so violent, as she would never talk about what might be wrong. It got so bad that Alex started to hit back, although as her mother was stronger she still got hurt. When she was thirteen her mother went away one day and didn't reappear. When over a week had passed, Alex got frightened and rang the police. They immediately took her to her present home as a temporary arrangement, but by the time they found her mother, Alex didn't want to go back to her and said so quite definitely. Fortunately, she was able to stay with her foster family, and at last has found a happy home. She sees her mother occasionally, but never wants to live with her again.

'It's really different having such a large family. It's great. There's always someone there. Most of us stay in during the week, or if we want to go somewhere, we've got our sisters and brothers to go out with. Most of us get on well, and if you're upset there's always someone there to cheer you up. It's nice to know you've got a family like that; we've got a shoulder to lean on.

I've only been there two years but Sheila knows me like the palm of her hand. She knows if there's anything wrong and I trust her a lot. She's a really kind of down-to-earth mother. I can treat her more like one of my friends than my mother. We have a mother-and-daughter relationship in certain respects, like she still puts her foot down here and there, but when we go out shopping together we act as if we're sisters. She's so young-looking, she dresses like we do, she's really trendy. I've always wanted a mum like that, who will just talk about anything; she knows all about the boyfriends I've had. She trusts me to act the way I'm supposed to, and to respect myself, and I respect her for that as well. It's the same with my dad; we're more like really good friends. He'll sit down and say, "Look, I don't think you should really be doing this," and then we sit and have a discussion about it. I've never wanted a dad before so I haven't actually thought of what I wanted my dad to be like.

He's the kind who likes us to learn by our mistakes, he doesn't stop us from doing everything. They treat me like a human being. I'm somebody, not just a body walking around. That's why I get on so well with them.

If I do something wrong and Sheila shouts at me I never ever answer back, because my family's African and you're taught never to answer back to your elders. The only person I answer back to is my real mum. If someone treats me like a piece of rubbish, like my mum does, then I would answer them back. Sheila says I'm really independent now, so she's treating me more like an adult. Like tonight I'll be going to the pub and meeting my friend, and after that we go to nightclubs and I can stay out to what time I want. When I go out late I always get a taxi back. Sometimes I do stupid things, and Sheila says to me, "If you want to be treated like an adult, you can't do that." So I know when I'm acting immature because she grounds me, and I think: my God, it's so shameful being grounded at sixteen!

In my third year at school I used to truant, and I got in trouble and had letters sent home. I used to get caught smoking, I never used to do my homework, and I got really bad marks. I wasn't allowed a lot of freedom then. Then when I got in the fifth year, I was told how serious this year was, and I just settled down completely. During the week I wouldn't go out at all, I spent three hours doing homework and I was never late for school. I did really well and all my teachers noticed a big change in me. I'm not the person I was before. I got seven GCSEs. But I'm sure I wouldn't have got them if it hadn't been for Sheila and Peter.

What we do about helping around the house is that we've got a rota for the dishwasher. We had a rota for all different things, but it just went completely wrong. My mum does the shopping and cooking, and if we all do a bit it helps her. She doesn't let us help with the cooking, she doesn't like people under her feet. But when she's making cakes, we fight over licking the bowl. If she's not well my dad always does it and he's a really good cook. We get £3.30 pocket money every Saturday, plus £6 clothing allowance. It comes from the Social Services, and when they don't send our money Sheila gives it to us out of her own money. She sees us as her own children, so if we want anything and we haven't got the money, she'll buy it for us and we'll pay her back. Some people think: well, she's your mum, why are you paying her back? But she's got to look after the house and feed ten of us every day. It's not easy. When we use the telephone we always give her ten pence, because her and my dad have to pay the phone bill, electricity and gas, and we all use these.

I've got a couple of black friends, but most of my friends are white. It's mainly because I've lived more with white people; it was always white people that fostered me. Sheila loves black children. Joseph was the only one she had, and then I came along, so we used to both get spoilt. Now we get treated like everyone else, but she still treats us a bit special sometimes. She gets me my own shampoo because I can only use a certain sort, and she's always telling me to cream my skin and things like that. Sheila doesn't like the way a lot of black people are treated. When we sit down and talk, we sometimes talk about apartheid and Nelson Mandela; I feel really strongly on all things like that. My mum's a mixture of Spanish, South American and Irish, she doesn't really act like a white person, she's kind of more black than I am! Sometimes I think to myself that I don't like being black because of the trouble that's happening but she always reassures me and says, "You should be proud to be black. Black is beautiful." It makes me feel so much better.

The Social Services did their best to get me to go back to a black family; they didn't think a white family was suitable. I think that's really stupid – how do they know where I'd be better off? My experience with my own family isn't very nice. It doesn't matter what colour the people are, it's wherever the child is comfortable. So I said I wasn't moving. We all dug our heels in. They tried to do the same with Joseph, but he didn't want to go either, so they've left it now. In a way I think it's a bit racist, like saying you shouldn't be with them because they're white. It's only the colour of the skin that makes us different, deep down everyone's the same. I was really going on and on about it so I think they got a bit bored with me, so they said, "Okay, you can stay there."

There's no difference made between us and Sheila and Peter's own children, and it's funny when we go out together and they say, "This is my sister." People always believe it for Nita because she's white, then they look at me and say, "How the hell can she be your sister?" We have to say, "We're fostered." Then they say, "Oh, so she's not your real sister." But we don't say that, we all see each other as real brothers and sisters. When Tony and me go out together they believe it, because he's half Portuguese and really dark-skinned. We always say we're real brother and sister. And if there's anything wrong the others come and say, "Look, I'm your sister, or I'm your brother, so chat to me" sort of thing. My brothers drive me mad sometimes, they wind me up, and sometimes I don't really want to talk to them. It's all part of having brothers, I suppose, but I get on better with my sisters, and we go places together.

Me and Nita have little chats about sex, and when we were on holiday Sheila gave us a big lecture about it. She'd say to the boys, "If you're going to have sex, please use condoms." And they'd laugh and go all red and say, "Yes, of course we will." And she'd say to us, "Make sure you carry a condom around with you in case the boys haven't, or go on the Pill, whichever one you want." Mum talks to us about things like that, and if we wanted to go on the Pill we'd discuss it with her first. We're always having discussions about AIDS as well; I think it's important for all parents to talk to their children about AIDS, even if they already know about it.

The best thing about my family is being able to laugh together. We've got a really big dining table and sometimes we all sit round it having a big chat and taking the mickey out of people. If it's a rainy day and you don't want to go out, you've always got your family there in the sitting room. We watch videos, or we play each other's music and exchange records or tapes. Because we're all around the same age, it makes it even better, we can talk about the same things. The worst thing is when someone does something to upset you and you try and explain it to them and they don't listen. It doesn't happen that much, just now and then. And what I hate most is when someone gets my mum or dad annoyed and they know they've done something bad but they're so stubborn they can't go up and say sorry.

I think a happy family is where everybody cares for everybody else. If someone does something good in your family and you say to them, "That's nice what you did", and they say the same to you. Whatever trouble you have, you work it out together. If you know someone is upset, you can think, "I know what will cheer her up," and you just do it. If someone says a joke about you, not taking it seriously, just laughing at it. And learning to keep control if someone gets on your nerves. Of course we have our ups and downs, every family does, but we always pull together, which makes us quite a happy family.

Sometimes when my real mother gets into a bit of bother I feel responsible for her, I feel that if I were there it wouldn't have happened. Sheila used to tell me not to feel that because I'd never get on with my own life, so now I don't. Anything that happens to my mum is her own business. When she rings up and tells me things I just say, "Oh, really". I don't feel responsible for her any more. She wanted to send me to Africa, so Sheila made me a ward of court, which meant my mum couldn't move me from that address, no matter what she did. But one thing I do like about her – and she's always done this since I was a baby – is on my birthday she always buys me a birthday cake, and a card.

I feel very bitter about not having had a family life before. Sometimes when Sheila says, "I remember when this lot were younger . . .", it makes me wish I'd lived here from the age of seven. But I can't be grumpy, I'm happy with what I've got. I think they're the best family I could wish for, and even though they drive me mad sometimes, I still love them. I can stay with Sheila and Peter as long as I want, probably until I'm about eighteen, or twenty, until I get a flat. I'm not too bothered about it. Sheila says there will always be room in the house for me, my bedroom will always be my room, so I don't need to move out. I hope I'll know them all my life. I don't think we'll ever drift apart; no matter where I end up I'll always go and see them. They're my real parents as far as I'm concerned.'

4

Holding
it Together

Making ends meet: Gwyn
Losing a brother: Janette

When the family is threatened it may fragment into pieces, or it
may become more united. Gwyn and Janette, who illustrate this
chapter, have had quite different experiences, but they are both
helping their families to hold things together. For Gwyn, it is the
effects of her parents trying to make ends meet. In today's society
everyone is encouraged to borrow money and buy houses, cars,
televisions, videos, washing machines, dishwashers, computers and
other trappings of our technological age. Anyone would think
people have all become better off over the last few years, but it's
not true. What has really happened is that the rich have got richer
and the poor have got poorer. Families have been encouraged (or
forced, where there's little or no rented accommodation left) to buy
houses, and then their wages can't keep pace with rising mortgage
payments. Lots of money doesn't necessarily bring happiness, but
not having enough can create conflict and anxiety within families,
and can break up marriages. Poverty is a common characteristic of
single-parent families, and as one sixteen-year-old said: 'I believe if
we were in no financial trouble we would have fewer rows. Nobody
can argue otherwise with me about that. Mum really tries hard and
can't afford anything for herself. I love her for that.' In Gwyn's
family, money troubles have taken their toll, but the family has so
far remained firmly and positively together.

For Janette, the experience that has devastated her family is the
sudden death of her brother. Losing someone so close is not easy
to think about, but it happens. If you cast your mind around all the

43

families you know, there is invariably at least one which has suffered some fatal tragedy. Sometimes it's after a long illness, so it's less of a shock, but it's just as hard to adjust to. It usually creates an emptiness within the family for which it's very hard to compensate. For Mandy, at fourteen, it was a huge shock when her mother died. As an only child she was having a comfortable and happy life:

> Then one day my mum died. She went out and never came back, it was a heart attack. It left just me and my dad; he was surrounded by grief and shut me out. It created a void between us, something that still exists today. I felt scared, vulnerable, confused and totally alone. I really loved my mum and it seemed I lost my dad's love the day my mum died.

Lisa (in Chapter 8) also lost her mother through sudden illness, and both she and Janette were initially left with overwhelming feelings of disbelief which still exist in Janette's family, even though it's eighteen months since her brother died. Each deals with her grief differently. Lisa tries not to think about it and gets on with life. Janette did too at first, but eventually broke down, and now advises talking and letting things out, however painful this may be. She and her mother get support from talking to a counsellor and her mother joined a group of mothers who had lost children in a similar way.* It's also important to explore any regrets and guilt. Children often feel they must have somehow contributed to the death of someone very close by some way they've acted or something they've said, and this can fester away for many years if it's not brought out into the open. It's very hard to cope with losing someone you love, but life does go on, there's still happiness to be found, and if you're young you have a future of your own to forge.

GWYN

Fourteen-year-old Gwyn lives in a small Welsh town with her parents, her sister, aged twelve, and her seven-year-old

---

* In some places, CRUSE, which is a support organisation for people who are suffering from the death of close loved ones, have set up a YOUNG CRUSE group, for children and young people. See the Contacts section.

*brother. They've had some rough times during which her
mother has suffered from depression, and her father has had
a nervous breakdown from the pressures of his job and from
getting into debt to pay their mortgage. She feels the whole
family have never fitted in anywhere, and this, combined with
everything else, has drawn them closer together. She and her
sister even used to have their own special language. They
moved to their present home four years ago, and Gwyn hates
it. She finds the people unfriendly, and she has little in
common with other girls at school. She'd sometimes like to
rebel, but in general her social life revolves around home.
Eventually she hopes to take drama at A level and go to
university or art college.*

'I used to have best friends, but none since we came up here. I've
got people I'm friendly with but they're all so teenagery and
teenybopperish. It's horrible saying that, but it's true. I think it's
because I've spent so much time talking with my mum and dad that
I can't really talk to people of my own age. I hated it here at first, I
didn't know anyone and no one seemed to want to know me. People
patronised me a bit; they went round with me but they didn't like
me. I've never really felt at home.

My sister and I are quite close as we have to share a room, but I
probably wouldn't like a room of my own. When she went away for
a week on a school trip I felt really lonely and she was homesick as
well. I wasn't expecting that, I'd thought it might be a relief. We
have a private language and if we're with different types of people,
stupid people like the lad across the road from us, we're always
making fun of him with private jokes and no one knows. When we
were little we used to gabble away and no one knew what we were
talking about. We had this game with imaginery people, like Lara,
Susan, John and Peter, that was really funny. But we stopped doing
that when we came here, with getting older and growing up. We
felt a bit out of place and we didn't like to do it. Now my sister's
getting older she wants to be apart from me more, and that's a bit
strange. She's always been sort of "my sister" and now she's getting
older she's becoming her own person. We're still as close as we
were, we just don't go around together as much as we used to.

We've had quite a few crises with money; we've only got enough
to live on from week to week. We can live comfortably, but not that

45

comfortably. We don't struggle for food or anything and we've got a decent house, but my mum was very upset because I didn't have one proper outfit to wear, and we were dyeing all my clothes, trying to convert them. Mum hates getting herself clothes, she feels guilty about that. I say, "That would suit you, Mum," and she says, "I can't get it, I have to get you clothes." I feel very sorry for her that she hasn't got enough clothes. I always say she can borrow mine but she doesn't like to do that, she feels that they're part of me. I really needed a coat and boots a couple of weeks ago – my clothes had just totally worn out – so Dad took me into town and got these. That's why I want to get a Saturday job because I'm getting money off them all the time and I feel a bit guilty about it. Me and my sister only get one pound pocket money a week, and I just discovered that my mum and dad have sold their wedding rings. I didn't believe things like that happened, it's so clichéd, but it's true!

Mum and Dad get really upset about us not having a car. It gets really horrible being stranded. A car would be really useful. My dad wouldn't have to get the bus to work and he could give me lifts to places. He's been ill lately, with his back, and I didn't want him to come and meet me, so I scrounged lifts off people. That was horrible. Dad nearly had a breakdown because of money, and his work. There were loans to pay off and bills to pay. It was like a vicious circle: the more loans he paid off, the more he was in debt because he borrowed from somewhere else. It had all got on top of him and I knew something was wrong. He was off work for three months. My dad has a horrible job, pestering people for tax. He hates doing things like that, he's very gentle. Now he's managing to treat it as just his job, he's coping with it more. He's in for promotion but he doesn't want to be promoted because he'll be an inspector, being tougher and harder and stamping on people. Even though it's more money, he says he couldn't be that ruthless. It upsets him, not having enough money, especially around Christmas time, but I wouldn't want him to go through what he's already been through by having a worse job.

Mum got ill when I was eight, after she had my brother James. She was taking tablets and they weren't the right ones for her. It was frightening because she used to hallucinate sometimes. She had these feelings that Dad didn't want her any more, and that was horrible. Once I rushed down to tell my dad, and she went to me,

"Oh, you're taking your dad's side now." It wasn't like her at all. Then she had to go back in hospital and I didn't know why and I began to blame it on my brother a bit. I was about twelve when all the after-effects were gone and Mum could talk about it with me. I think that's helped to make us close, going through that.

Mum stayed at home looking after me, then my sister came along so she looked after her, then she hurt her back so she couldn't go out to work, and then she had James. She feels guilty that she can't go out to work, but she doesn't like the idea of working mothers and my dad's the same. He's always saying about people who go out to work and leave their children with child-minders. I don't know what I think. I suppose you should be independent, but I don't think she'd enjoy working. She'd be wondering how we were at school, things like that. She doesn't like other people looking after us. She goes out to the shops and that, but she and dad don't go out at night. My dad doesn't drink, so there's not many places for them to go, so they stay at home in front of the telly. Sometimes I get fed up with them being in, but I'm used to it. It got on my nerves after a while when my dad was at home all the time, as I have a different relationship with my mum when my dad's there. I don't know why, but I don't really want to intrude when he's around. So me and my sister have never really made a habit of hanging around downstairs. The living room is where we all congregate. We have our meals and sometimes watch television; the rest of the time we're in our room.

My mum and dad are a perfect couple; they've got a lot in common and a lot different and they complement each other. They've stuck to each other for ages, through everything, and that makes us closer. My sister can't talk to them the way I do, but sometimes I've felt that they didn't confide enough in me when there was a problem. A lot of times my dad has come home looking really upset and Mum and Dad go into their room and shut the door and I can hear them crying. I don't know what it's about, but it's always to do with money. They like to be private like that. They never tell me when there are bad financial problems. There are a lot of secrets they have that I never know about, and I think that's the main problem between me and them. I know they don't want to worry me but I get even more worried when I know something's going on and they won't tell me. Then they ask me what I'm worried about! I can't ask, I feel it's a bit nosey, but now I'm getting older I feel more responsible.

I think I'm older than my age in some senses, like I know more about money matters and how the world works, and I don't really trust many people; my dad always said don't ever tell any confidence unless it's someone you can really trust. But in other ways I'm younger because I'm not allowed out at night and I don't go to many parties. People have invited me, but they're usually the sort my mum and dad wouldn't want me to go with. Usually I make up stories and say I can't go because my gran's coming round or something. I don't really want to go, it's not my sort of thing, being dead loud and getting drunk. I've never been drunk in my whole life. Sometimes I've wanted to do it for the hell of it, to see what Mum and Dad would do, but it would hurt them – especially my dad, he doesn't like drink. Sometimes I've gone out and told them I've gone somewhere else, but I don't enjoy it because I feel guilty. And we don't really do anything, just walk around and shout things at people, get into a fight or chase lads. So in the evenings I stay in, listen to music – mostly my dad's LPs or some stuff on the radio – and do my homework. I write stories and plays.

At times I wish I had a bit more freedom, like if my dad's in a mood that he won't let me go out, then I get a bit angry, but usually I'm content with it. Sometimes they don't let me go to places on my own; my dad walks me and that irritates me because I don't want to be seen with him. He doesn't like the idea of me having a boyfriend, he says boys are all after one thing, he doesn't really want me to grow up. Mum's all right, she had a very strict upbringing and wants me to have more freedom. But I just want to be myself, and not have any expectations made of me.

In a way we're a middle-class family, as we live in a middle-class area, but always with the sort of people who look down on us. I hate middle-class people; I don't want to be like them. The people in our street – one day they're talking to us and the next day they're not. I don't know why. Maybe because Mum and Dad don't have a holiday and don't have a car they think they're a bit stingy and that I'm strange because I'm not like a teenybopper. My dad was a bit like me at my age; he was a bit offbeat and didn't have many friends. I feel passionately about CND, Greenpeace, Animal Rights and Red Wedge. I don't feel I fit in, but I don't think I've ever fitted in anywhere. I don't really mind that much, people have to take me as they find me. My place is just home. I'm fed up with trying to conform to people, do what other people want me to do. I'm just with Mum and Dad now. That's my social circle. They're my real friends, and my sister and brother. I always know that they'll stick by me whatever. It's something I can't describe, the bond in my family.'

JANETTE

Janette was living happily with her parents and her brother Michael until eighteen months ago. Then their whole family life was turned upside down by Michael's death. It was totally unexpected, and the family is still recovering. Janette, who's sixteen now, was a year younger than her brother and they'd always got on well. When her dad was working late it would be her mother, Michael and herself together watching television, and she felt they were all very close. After Michael died she tried to carry on as normal, but she didn't like to talk about it at school, and didn't really grieve properly until months afterwards when it helped to talk to her mother's counsellor. Now she feels better about it but still, like her mother, can't quite believe that he's really gone.

'There seemed absolutely nothing wrong with Michael at all, but a couple of days before he died he was telling my mum that he had pains in his arms, so my mum sent him to the doctors. They thought it was exam nerves and gave him a prescription for an upset stomach. Mum thought that was wrong. That was on the Friday, then on Monday he left for school ten minutes before me and everything was as usual. When I came home from school Mum and Dad were both in, which was unusual, but I didn't think anything of it. Then Mum was crying as she told me what had happened. She hadn't wanted to ring me at school, she wanted to tell me herself.

Michael was in school playing football when the ball went over a wall into the convent. He said, "I've got a pain in my heart," and suddenly fell to the ground. One of the boys with him got a nun out of the convent, and a passer-by tried to give him the kiss of life. They got the ambulance but he died when he got to the hospital.

My mum can't really believe it because he went out okay in the morning — how could anything like that happen? It was just a virus, like a one-in-a-million chance, and it affected his heart. He was brought home and stayed here a couple of days before he was buried. I don't remember any of that at all. I think I blocked it out and I still can't face up to it. Neither can my mum. She goes to the cemetery every other day, but she says she feels she's not standing there alone, and that's how I feel. Even after a year and six months I just don't think he's dead. I don't feel that he'll come back, but I don't feel that he's gone for ever. We were very close. We had arguments and fought like any other brother and sister, but I don't feel guilty about anything. The thing I miss most is his friendship. Michael was a lot cleverer than me and he helped me with things I didn't understand, like my school problems with maths and things. I think he would have gone to university.

Life has really changed, everything's changed. My mum said she'd never go on another holiday, not abroad, because we used to go abroad every year. And last Christmas she wouldn't put up a Christmas tree or anything like that. But I didn't want that either, it just wasn't the same. What was there to celebrate? But I think we're going to celebrate it this year. Just before it happened we were going to move house, but Mum would never move now. And at first she didn't even want to get the house redecorated because she wanted it to stay the same as it was, but in the end she changed her mind and I think she's glad she did. But Michael's room has stayed exactly the same, with all his school books and things, she'll never change that. She said, "I'll go through them one day." Each day she goes in there because she feels that he's still in there. I hardly ever go in the room. It's like a fear, but I don't know what of. Since it happened the house is not the way it used to be; it's not gloomy, but it's not full of joy. I feel lonely quite a lot. I've got loads of friends, and I've got my mum and my nan and aunties and cousins, but something's missing.

At first I had to be a shoulder for Mum to cry on, because she had nobody then, as the counsellor didn't come straight away and she only started going to a women's support group six months ago. I'd like to be like my mum, the way she's looked after us. I respect her and Dad, and they respect me. I trust them and I think that's important. My relationship with my mum is like having a sister, and since Michael died we're even closer than we were before. We both like sewing and I help her with her sewing problems and she'll help me. We talk a lot; I tell her almost everything, except about sex and things because I'd get too embarrassed. I know when she's feeling depressed and I help her through it. If I'm at college and she hasn't been well, she bucks up a bit when I get home. Mum used to be a home help, but she never went back after Michael died because she couldn't face looking at old people when her son had just died. If she's sitting home all day she'll just sit and think, but if I'm at home or my dad's home we'll take her mind off it. She always says: why did it happen? And she's really bitter against anybody who ever hated Michael in any way, like he had a fight with a boy years ago and she remembers that.

After he died in May I tried to act normally. As far as I was concerned nothing had happened. I must have looked stupid to some people. I didn't know what to say and people didn't know what to say to me. Once I got into the swing of things again it seemed okay, but then Christmas came along. I suppose if somebody had asked me about it, it might have brought it on sooner, but nobody said anything in case they upset me. But then I got really bad, and I couldn't face the people at school. I cried for no reason at all, I didn't want to live, I wanted to die. I thought I was just depressed, but the counsellor said it was about Michael dying, and I was taking out my anger on the school, saying I hated the teachers and I didn't want to go in. I didn't go to school for about a month, and then it was hard the first day back, getting used to things again, but it felt a lot better. I think I just needed time to think. I don't know what it was but one minute I felt I couldn't go out and the next minute I felt I was going mad staying in all the time. I only went to my friend's or my nan's. Sometimes I still can't bear to stay in.

I'm at college now and that's much better, but I find it hard when people ask if I've got any brothers and sisters. I can't bring myself to tell them. When I used to make friends, that was a main question, but I wouldn't ask it because they'd ask me back and I dreaded that. Once a boy asked me a few months after Michael had died and I said, "No, I haven't got any." And so he was saying to me, "I'd love to be an only child, I think it's great." Eventually I did tell him, and I thought: if people ask, I've got to tell them, but I'll avoid the question if I can. My dad doesn't really say much about it either. He's a typical man – he won't say if he's upset. I think he's a bit like me, he likes to bottle it up, whereas my mum will just let it out. Mum talks to Dad, but sometimes I think he doesn't want to say anything to my mum in case he starts her off. I think everybody has their own way of coping with it. My mum hasn't really accepted it. From the start she cried all the time, whereas I didn't. I grieved a lot later. Mum feels she's got to have photographs around, but her friend who lost her son won't have any. And Mum likes to talk about it, because she thinks if people don't, they're sweeping it under the carpet.

If it happened to someone else, I'd say: don't force your feelings. Just cope with it the way you feel. If you feel you don't want to cry, don't cry, it will come in time. And don't feel bad if you don't want to talk about it. Sometimes I was like that, because I didn't want to believe it. I felt shocked when Michael died but I didn't feel guilty that we fought like cat and dog; that was part of our relationship. I often used to think I was going mad, I thought that nobody felt like me. I felt as if I hated everybody, and I hated people talking about it. I used to think: they've got no right. This feeling came and went and came and went again. I don't think I'd feel like that now, although I still find it hard to talk to people outside the family about it. I talk to my mum, or my nan, people who really knew him. I think a time will come when I will be able to talk about it openly. Everything seems to be "If only, if only", but you can't really live like that. I think it's made me grow more responsible and face things, and I keep busy now. If you sit and think, you work yourself into a depression. I do think about Michael a lot and he comes into the conversation every day.

There's no such thing as a happy family. I think there's a semi-happy family, and that's what we are. But we're not really a family any more, because a chunk's gone. There's the three of us but it doesn't feel like a family, because a family was my mum, dad and us two. I don't think we'll ever be a family again because he's not going to come back, is he? But there again, maybe as I get used to it I'll see it in a different light.'

5

Mothers and Daughters

Closer without Dad: Angela
A clash of personalities: Ellie
More a friend than a mother: Patricia

Mothers and daughters have always had intense relationships. It's a subject often written about and a source of constant conversation amongst girls and women of all ages. With mothers you can share lots of things – from feelings and emotions to clothes and make-up. Getting on with your mother can be like a rollercoaster. It seems to go up and down and sometimes churn you around inside. And it can change from year to year, especially as you move through your teens. Because mothers have been daughters, they have been through some of what you may be going through – like starting periods, getting interested in boys, feeling moody and depressed – and they can be helpful and sympathetic – or they might not! Women tend to be much more open about their feelings than men, and it's usually easier to talk about personal things to mothers rather than fathers. But this has another side: such close loving can implicitly demand things from you in return, which can make you feel guilty if you don't do what is expected. Being the same sex as your mother also means you are both more likely to identify with each other, which is nice but may make it harder for you to separate and find your own identity. Emotions can run in all directions, but whatever happens she is still your mother and you can't help but be strongly affected by her.

Most girls who wrote to me had good or reasonably close relationships with their mothers. Patricia describes hers as a very happy family; she gets on very well with both parents and treats her mother more like a friend. But mothers and daughters can clash through being too alike, or they may have conflicting personalities or views. Ellie had got on well with her mother until her early teens, when they grew radically apart. They each feel hurt by one another and their relationship is mutually upsetting.

If you live with one parent, your relationship with them becomes much more central. As you'll have noticed, about one family in every five is a one-parent family, and if your parents split up, chances are you'll end up living with your mother. This can be very tough financially, as women's pay is still generally lower than men's, and those relying on Income Support have only just enough to survive on. There's inevitably a drop in living standards, and things like holidays and cars may be out of the question. It can be hard trying to cope, especially in the first few years, but it can also closely unite mother (or father) and children. Problems are discussed and better understood, as in Jackie's family, where she lives with her mother and two brothers:

> It's very tough on the financial side but you've got to stick together. The good thing about living in a single-parent family is that you get to know that parent a lot more and understand what they're going through. The bad things are being constantly skint and not having a car or video.

Living with one parent also means children, and especially daughters, having to become more responsible for helping at home. This can feel good but it can be a lot of work, as fifteen-year-old Teresa shows: 'I cook the dinner every night, iron, wash the car and lots more, but I think it's fair as my mum works.' Experiences and feelings may also be more easily shared, and many girls living with their mothers have said how much closer they have become, how they confide in each other, ask one another's advice, and do more things together – like Michelle, aged eighteen: 'My mother says I help her have a younger outlook on life. She's fun and understanding, like a sister. I can talk to her about almost anything and she's very honest with me.' Angela also describes the relationship she has developed with her mother since her father left.

ANGELA

Angela lives in Scotland with her mother. Her parents divorced seven years ago, when she was six, and her memories of their unhappy and often violent life together still bring tears to her eyes. But since then, Angela and her mother have had a much happier life together, especially in the last few years. Her mother has resumed her education, and also has a part-time job. They have formed a close relationship, and Angela has strong views on single-parent families.

'I'm fed up with people feeling sorry for me. I'm glad my dad lives five hundred miles away! Adults who aren't victims of divorce are always saying how terrible it would be to lose a parent through divorce, but I don't think they have a right to comment on it if they've never been involved in it.

I'd better start at the beginning. My dad was very violent when he was drunk and he hit my mum. I suppose you could say she was a battered wife. I hate saying this but it's true. I used to dread the moment when he'd come in, swearing and shouting. I remember him hardly ever being in and my mum always looking sad. There was one night in particular, when Dad had come in drunk. He swore at my mum, then told me to get out of the room. But the wooden door couldn't block out the noise of my dad slapping and punching my mum. The memories are still very painful. Now I really hate my dad. He lives with his wife and two children. One he had the cheek to call Angela and the other Susan – my mum's name.

My parents divorced when I was six, and my mum and I went to my gran's house for two years. I hated living there because my gran's really nosey so I didn't have any privacy at all. Mum and I shared a bed, it must have been terrible for her. But that all changed when we got a house of our own, five years ago. It's much better – I have my own room, furniture I like, and everything is modern.

Mum works a few evenings a week as a clerical officer and goes to university to study English and Scottish literature in the daytime, which she really enjoys. I'm very proud of her, and she's proud of me too because I get good marks at school. Mum and I have a very

55

open relationship and my friends envy me for that. I think the divorce has brought us closer. She's always there for me when I come home from school and I always enjoy dinner time. Even if mum's working from five to nine we always have dinner together. She tells me about her day and I tell her about mine. We talk easily about lots of things. At night over supper we always talk about sex. Mum tells me about her old boyfriends and how her parents didn't let her do things like staying out late and going out with boys. She tells me that she wants me to be much freer than she was when it comes to things like that. Mum says she married my dad because at sixteen she was allowed to see boys and my dad was the first one that came along! She says she just wanted to be free from her parents. I've been out with a few guys, but never anything serious. Right now I've lost interest in boys. I can't be bothered with them. I tell my mum everything, just about, and she tells me private things as well and treats me as an equal adult. She tells me about her relationship with her boyfriend and asks my advice on lots of things.

Sometimes being in a one-parent family can be bit of a nuisance. For example, at school yesterday someone asked me what I was getting my dad for Christmas. And when you say, "I haven't got a dad," the questions start, then sympathy and then more questions. But I'm not in that situation very often. Living in a single-parent family is great for me, but it isn't for my friend who lives with her dad and his girlfriend. She says she can't talk to her dad because he's a male and she hates his girlfriend. He doesn't even know she's had her periods for a year and a half!

I think marriage is a very big commitment. Too many people just rush into it without thinking carefully. They just want to be with their partner all the time. For the rest of their lives they would be with one person. When you go to sleep, when you wake up, at breakfast (you'd probably need to cook it for him!) he'd always be there. At lunch, at dinner, at supper, when you're watching TV, you can't avoid him. And you certainly couldn't go anywhere near another man. Some people do consider all these things but they assume that the love they have for their boyfriend will be the answer for everything. Just now I feel that I never want to get married unless I have lived with my partner for a couple of years and still love him. I probably feel like this because I have witnessed a marriage fall apart. My mum hadn't even lived with my dad at all and she'd only known him for six months. When I asked my mum if she had married my dad because she was pregnant she said she would have married him anyway because she loved him. Mum's an excellent example of someone who just didn't think about the future!

During divorce I think the children should be well informed and nothing should be kept from them. I think children should be given a say in who gets custody of them. After all, it is the children who are in the middle of it all. Parents can't just say, "Leave this to Mum and Dad. It's got nothing to do with you." I think the success of a single-parent family really depends on a lot of things. The parent becomes a very close friend, someone to confide in, not just someone who looks after you. Divorce separates the two adults but brings the children and the adult they live with together. You've got to pull together and make the most of what you've got. Being an only child makes all that much easier. I would hate to have brothers or sisters because I would need to share my mum with them. My mum's completely changed since divorcing my dad. She doesn't worry as much as she used to. She also has a better social life and has had a boyfriend for six years. Divorce is a very sad thing but very necessary if the marriage is going downhill fast. For me and my mum, this was definitely the best thing.'

ELLIE

Ellie's mother was sixteen, the same age as Ellie, when she ran away to live with her boyfriend, and seventeen when she got pregnant. She left without telling him she was having a baby, and when Ellie was born, decided that she had no means to look after her. Ellie was taken into care, but her grandparents found out and she went to live briefly with them. It didn't work out, so she was fostered in various homes before finally being adopted, aged three, by the Yorkshire family that she has been with ever since. She often wonders about her real mother and father. She was very happy until her early teens, when things began to go wrong between her and her adoptive mother. She's always had a closer relationship with her father.

'I've always known I was adopted. I know my real mum was only seventeen when she had me, and if I was in her place I would have done the same thing. I've got this report that my dad gave me and it tells all my history, and it says that my real mum wouldn't tell my real dad what happened, she never wanted to see him again. She won't even give his name. I don't think it's fair on me and I don't think it's fair on him. He's got a daughter out there and he doesn't even know. If only she sent me a photo, I just want to know what he looks like. I know he's a lorry driver and he's supposed to be tall, dark-haired, with grey eyes. When we're on the motorway going on holiday, if I see a lorry with a tall, dark-haired driver I think, "That's my dad!" To this day I don't agree with her not telling my dad. Even if he said, "I don't care, I don't want to know her," that's his choice, but I'm a part of him and I don't know him, not even his name. From the report I know my mum was five foot six inches tall and had long dark hair, brown eyes, long legs and everything. I'm just coming up to the age that my mother had me and I think about it a lot. Every birthday I wonder, "Will she think about me today?"

My mum and dad, as I know them, had two sons, and they wanted a girl. Originally my dad was going to Vietnam to get a little Vietnamese girl, then I came up and they adopted me. I've been happy really, but I know I've given them difficult times. I used to go everywhere with my mum. I wouldn't ever be separated from her. But I think it changed when I was about thirteen and went to senior school. I tried to grow up before my time. It's hard for me to explain in words. I think she wanted to keep me as her little girl. I know my dad still does, but with him there's not such tight restrictions. My dad was brilliant, we've always been close. I always go to my dad first before my mum, even with women's things. She's more interested in my brother Paul. He's got his own business and she spends all her time there. She never seems interested in me at all now. I do know if anything happened to me then Jeff, Paul and my dad would be out there right away, but it's just my mum. I think it must be a clash of personalities. She thinks it's my fault, I think it's hers. If you talked to my mum now she'd probably give totally the other side of the story, saying that I don't make conversation with her. Maybe it's like that really. Even my friends notice it. My mates come up to my house and we have some tea and they've said to me, "What's wrong with you and your mum?"

and I say, "What do you mean?" "You never talk, never have a conversation."

My being adopted came into arguments a lot of the time, but never with my dad. I know it's in the back of my mind that he's not my real dad, but he's the one who's brought me up. Whereas my mum would say, "You're not doing this, you're not doing that," and I'd say, "You're not my mother, you never gave birth to me." All that sort of thing. Then my brother Paul would come in saying, "Don't talk to your mum like that." And I'd say, "You're not my brother either." When I was going through a bad patch I always used to bring it up, and resent it. In one way, being adopted makes you feel: it's brilliant, they chose me; but you've always got the other side – that your mother didn't want you. I know I say I don't get on with my mum and everything but I'd never ever put my real mum before my mum, it wouldn't be right.

I think the baddest of the bad times started with Iqubal, although it was bad before then. He was just eighteen when I started going out with him, and I was fourteen. I knew they objected to him and we had arguments about it. I wanted to rebel against my parents. I wouldn't do anything they wanted and looking back on it I knew it was totally out of order. One evening we'd arranged to hire a telly and get some videos to watch round at my friend's boyfriend's flat. I told my dad I was at Alison's and she told her mum she was staying at my house. Everything was fine and we had a brilliant laugh. Later in the week, Alison rang me up to say her mum had found her diary. I thought: my God, she'll tell my dad everything, but I went to meet Iqubal as usual and came back and there was Alison's mum. It all came out and the diary got flashed about to everybody. After Alison's mum went home, my mum went to bed and it was just me and my dad. He said, "I read that Alison went with you to Family Planning and you're on the Pill and sleeping with him." After Iqubal and I had been going out for six months, I'd gone on the Pill, but I said, "No. She's lying. She's just got a good imagination. It's not true." I wouldn't admit it at all, but he'd already been in my room and found all my pills. He said, "What are these, then?" and started crying. He was ever so upset, he went literally white. I knew it was illegal. I was underage, but I'd been going with him ages and he was the first I'd slept with. I thought: it's up to me what I do with myself. I said, "All right, I'm on the

Pill." I didn't know what else to do. He said, "Right, if you sleep with him before you're sixteen, it's police and everything."

I think Dad was upset because I was only fifteen and on top of that Iqubal was a Pakistani. If I'd got pregnant it would be a mixed-culture baby, which I'm not bothered about, but my dad's got different views. Dad's still very protective over me, although not so much because Iqubal went back to Pakistan about six months ago. I don't know if it's just me or it's got something to do with rebelling against the family, but personally I think dark-coloured blokes are nicer than white ones. I seem to be attracted to them more. My mum and dad don't like it but they know there's no way they can really stop me. I thought I loved Iqubal and he told me he loved me, but looking back now I realise it was a very big mistake. I've grown up a hell of a lot since I've left home.

I was good at school, I know if I'd never met Iqubal I could have got A's in every subject, but I took his attitude. He was two years above me and very cheeky to the teachers. I ran away from home about four times. First time it was about a week; second time six days; third time about four days. The fourth time I couldn't really say it was running away, it was just one night and I went to my friend's. Then one day when I was sixteen I was getting ready for school, and I wanted to wear some particular trousers. It was after Iqubal had gone, so I was getting on better with my mum. I said, "Mum, can you iron these trousers?" We had an argument but she said, "All right, I'll do them." But the iron was too hot and she scorched them. You could see the tiniest outline of the iron. I went up the wall, and we had this massive row, the worst I've ever had, and my dad came down. I can remember him saying, "Get out of this house, you upset your mum and me so much!" So I just went. I knew one of my friends wasn't going to school that day so I went to the phone box and called her. Her mum's good on things like that so I met them in town. Her mum said to go to this counselling place that deals with things like that. So I did, and got a place that afternoon, in lodgings. It was in a big block of flats in not a very good area, but I didn't care. I thought: I've got a place of my own, it's going to be brilliant. I can do what I want now.

I had to get a letter from my dad saying he gave me permission to live away from home because I was under eighteen. After two or three months the people moved so I went to live in a bedsit in a house owned by a friend of my dad. At first I was getting Income

Support, but that didn't go anywhere so I got a job in a supermarket. But you can only earn about £5 before they start deducting it from your benefit, so it ended up I was working fifteen hours a week for an extra £6, and in the end I thought: it's not worth it. I left and went on a YTS computing course. I think when I did leave home I had to grow up to be able to look after myself, like to survive, and it made me appreciate my home more.

A few months ago I moved back, and I think what eventually made me go home was I was having trouble with the rent, plus my brother's wedding had been the week before, which had upset me. Most of the time I had tears in my eyes, especially at the reception. I was so happy that the whole family was there and everyone was getting on brilliant, and me and Mum got on fantastic all day and I thought: I'm missing out. But what really put the topping on it was, I had a telly and one day the TV licence people came and I hadn't got a licence. I managed to persuade them to give me three weeks to get one. I told my dad I'd have to bring the telly back and collect it in a couple of weeks, and explained why. The next morning there was an envelope addressed to me. My dad had bought me a TV licence. Added to this, he gave me £100 to go and buy some things when I started the YTS course, because I was on this placement and I had to be smart. So I thought: it's not right, he's giving me all this money, but he's never asked me to come home because he knew it would put me in an uncomfortable situation. So I decided to go back.

On the male side of the family, we all get on much better now. But my mum and me, although we got on ever so well for the first few weeks, then little things started up and now we're picking faults with each other. And if she's ever in before I come home there's never anything like "Had a nice day at work? Are you going out tonight?" I just get the impression that she doesn't want to hear. On the outside I don't like my mum the way she is, and she could say the same about me. But on the inside I know she's the best mum I could have. It's hypocritical in a way. There's no give and take. We both take, neither of us gives. There's times I just sit in my bedroom, I want to scream and shout my head off. I want to get hold of her, shake her and say, "Why can't you take notice of me?" but I know it will never come to that. I'll just storm upstairs and my dad will come up, saying, "What's going on? Why can't you compromise?" But I just won't go downstairs and say, "Look Mum,

I'm sorry, can we start again?" I've tried it before and it didn't work, so I've given up now.'

PATRICIA

Patricia is nearly eighteen and lives in London with her parents and her brother, who's almost fifteen. Her parents met and married here, after coming to England from Ireland when they were teenagers. Her mother was very pleased to have Patricia, because she'd been told she couldn't have children. But then Patricia came along, followed by her brother. Her mother works as a nanny to a barrister's family, and her father works in a television props department. Patricia is doing A levels and hopes to study law at university. She and her parents get on well, and they still all enjoy going on holiday together. She and her brother each take a friend and do their own things; they stay out very late, then all meet up and talk about what they've done. Compared with her other friends, this sharing relationship with her parents seems quite unusual. There's only one thing that they have found they disagree on.

'I'm so happy with my family. My mum is my best friend and I confide everything in her. She is understanding, liberal and she considers my wishes as well as her own. My mother's more like a grown-up friend – the best mum in the world! I also get on with my father brilliantly. He allows me my independence and freedom and we deeply respect each other's views. He doesn't play the over-protective father role yet cares considerably, which means arguments are very rare. We talk about absolutely everything. They take a real interest in what me and my brother do, and my friends – not just at school but other things. My friends envy us together because they can't seem to talk to their parents. It's not that they don't get on, but they treat them like parents. It's the way they treat us, quite leniently, we're quite free to do what we want. They trust us and respect us and we tell them what we're doing.

My mum and dad get on extremely well, although they're different in that my dad's quiet and my mum's very loud, she's the active one. He'll always agree with my mum, he won't go against her. He doesn't get quite as involved as my mum. When they first got married they never had much of a social life; now they're out all the time. We don't do many social things together, but what my friends find quite interesting is that if we've been out for an evening or if they've been out, we'll come back in and all sit in the kitchen together, I don't just stay in one room with my friends. They find that really funny, because my mum and dad are joining in as if they were teenagers and everyone thinks: I wish my mum and dad were like that. My mum and dad are quite childish at heart. My friends really like my parents because they treat them as equals, they don't treat them as kids or talk down to them. At times they seem to share the same mentality as us, although my mum's forty-four and my dad's fifty-three! They're young at heart in a nice way.

My mum is really important to my friends too. They don't go directly to her, but I usually tell her about their problems anyway. She knows everything that's going on with me and my friends, and will pass an opinion or give some advice through me and I'll often say, "My mum said . . ." because they know that I usually tell her. My mother identifies with me a lot, like there was a big problem last year when my friend decided to go out with my boyfriend. My mum was really, really good. I spoke to the girl afterwards and we talked about it and the first thing she said was what did your mum think, and she decided to ring my mum up to say sorry for what she'd done to me.

My parents act like parents should in certain ways, like encouraging me to do well in education, and they're quite disciplined as well. They're not that liberated, but they've just got the right balance – very lenient when I need them to be but they're concerned with education, which I really like. I take their advice but totally reject any form of pressure to do well, it has to be of my own free will to work hard. I've got friends whose parents are far too lenient or far too disciplined and they usually go to extremes. They think that their mums don't trust them, that they seem to expect them to take advantage, and they go wild. Most of the things they don't want me to do I wouldn't want to do myself anyway.

I have a typical relationship with my younger brother. He and I have silly fights or we're bickering all the time over trivial things, but underneath it all we get on extremely well. At times I'm sure my mum thinks we really hate each other the way we shout at one another, but she doesn't understand. To us it doesn't really matter.

When we're apart we miss each other a lot. They were much more lenient with my brother than with me; it may be because he's a boy. My brother's not academically bright and they don't encourage him as much as they do me. He's more interested in learning a trade, doing something practical. My mum was very bright but she didn't have the opportunity because she lived in the country in Ireland, so she wants me to do as much as possible. She wants me to see as much of the world as I can and do as much as I can first. She realises how important it is for a girl to get an education, more so than for a boy, so even though my mum's happily married, she's put the idea of marriage while I'm young totally out of the window.

They never give me a moral guideline apart from sex before marriage, but I try to remain independently minded about the whole thing. They're Catholic so we're not expected to do it, although my mum's not very, very religious. But we do talk about it a lot; my mum and I will sit down and I'll tell her something that's happened. I know what my mum's going to say and she knows what I'm going to say, but we still say it. I always disagreed with my mum, because she was brought up in a different age and a different country. I used to think I just don't agree with her about sex before marriage and that was it, but as I'm getting older I'm getting to respect her views more. I'm not sure now. But I've never had a very serious boyfriend until now, so it's never arisen with me. My parents like my boyfriend, and he's not like that at all. I'm very lucky that he respects me. We've been going out for nearly three months. I'm not sure if I could tell her if I did do it. I think all hell would let loose! But I think it would all depend on who I was going out with too. In everything I do I take my mum's opinion into account. I may not do what she wants, but I always consider it.

Most of my friends have got serious boyfriends, they're on the Pill and having sex and my mum doesn't agree with it. They're not Catholics, but my friend who's Catholic, she didn't tell her mum she's on the Pill. I had to go with her for it, and to show the way they see my mum as so important, she knows I tell my mum everything but this was the one thing she begged me not to tell my mum and I never did. I think my mum assumes she is though. A lot of my friends have found out that their mothers were about two months pregnant when they got married, and they find it really funny. But I can't say that of my mum. She was a virgin when she got married, which makes me respect her because she practises what she preaches.

Mum talked to me about the facts of life when I was about eight, but I knew them already from my primary school. I couldn't bear to tell her that I knew already, so I played along with it. I could talk to her and to Dad about periods, we were quite open about that, and like if I'm in a bad mood from it. And like we have a communal bathroom, there might be four of us using the bathroom – one in the bath, one putting on make-up, Dad shaving, things like that. Although I think I did go through a stage, when I was about twelve, when I wanted to be private.

I don't think my family's different from others, they're not exceptionally liberated, it's just that they show things in a different way. All decisions are discussed and shared amongst the household. I don't get told what to do, everything is done fairly, based on mutual agreement. I am allowed to do virtually anything I wish within reason. But neither my brother or I do anything around the house. My brother's never in, and I'm really terrible. I just don't see it as one of my priorities. I hate anything domestic and my mum's never made me do it. I used to clean my room every Saturday but I've got my Saturday job now so I don't do that any more. But I'm a very tidy person, it's only things like dusting. We seem to have a role reversal in my family. I can't do anything domestic and my dad's very good at domestic things. If he's got a day off he'll do anything in the house, and he cooks quite well.

A happy family means co-operation between members, listening to reason, and giving continual emotional support. The best things about my family are we respect and consider each other's wishes, my brother and I have a lot of freedom, and we are very open and honest with each other. I think it's our parents having respect for us and we respect them, it's a give and take. It's getting the balance right.'

6

Loyalties

Stretching love to the limit: **Diane**
Living with violence: **Shelley**
Doing well for their sake: **Julie**
Let down when you need them most: **Ruth**

I started hating my mother when she started hitting me, but the thing that annoys me is that I know I still love her. She's my mum. It's just natural. Deep down, if anything were to happen to her I'd be really worried about her, but then I think of all the things she's done and I can't stand her. (Alex)

Families can provide a lot of security and support, and loyalty seems a simple thing to give in return. It's easy to do in a close family – like Gwyn's, for instance (in Chapter 4). But sometimes it's more difficult, and complicated by conflicting feelings of love and hate. Nobody's perfect, and most people can think of embarrassing occasions when they wish they or their parents would drop through the floor. But some parents do things that make family life constantly difficult or unbearable. Excessive drinking is one of these. Within the family, fathers are the main culprits, but not the only ones, and Jane's mother turned to drink when she was trying to decide whether to get a divorce (in Chapter 7). Unemployment and drinking don't have to go together, but they often do. and several girls talked about fathers who had lost jobs and now spent much of their time in the pub. The effects on the family can be very destructive, and Diane describes how it's stretching her love for her father to breaking point.

Drinking often leads to violence. The family provides the scene for many violent dramas, and battered wives and children have often featured in the news. In the 1970s the first women's refuges opened their doors, and Women's Aid has successfully campaigned to provide houses where women and children can be safe. Despite the publicity about family violence there is little evidence that it has become less frequent, and more than a few girls wrote to me describing incidents in which their parents had hit them, or each other. It can be hard to remain with people who are inflicting pain, but a strong family ideology of love and loyalty often ensures that people hold together for a long time. Women stay in violent situations for this reason, but also because they don't have enough money to live anywhere else, or they can't imagine an alternative, or they are afraid of being on their own. Shelley describes her parents' violent relationship and how it makes her feel about them.

Loyalty also plays a part in the way we often want to please our parents by doing what they want. It's part of the way a lot of girls are brought up. We are also pressured to be a 'good girl' in all sorts of ways. One of these is performing well – for instance, do they expect you to excel at school? Or be a genius on the piano or violin? Do they want you to have all the opportunities that they never had? Did your brother or sister mess up at school and they're relying on you to make up for it? It's great when you can, but a bit of a strain if you can't, and you end up feeling guilty that you're not fulfilling their hopes. Julie describes how her parents want her to do well in all the things their own parents could never afford to give them, and how she has tried to do her best to succeed for them.

Children often remain loyal to their parents through thick and thin, and should be able to expect the same in return. In Ruth's case, this didn't seem to be so. After it was revealed that she'd been sexually abused by her brother, she felt very betrayed that her parents did nothing about it. Child sexual abuse has been very much in the news over recent years, partly as a result of the Cleveland Inquiry, and it's clear that many children, and particularly girls, have been subjected to some sexual experience within the family. The Inquiry also prompted many adult women to tell, often for the first time, of childhood experiences they were too afraid to reveal before.

When you're young, it's hard to understand what's going on in such a situation, or to know what to do. You may feel quite powerless because the person involved is older or stronger, and has authority over you. It may even be someone you love and want to please. It's more often a man that's involved – he may be an uncle, father, stepfather, older brother or some family friend. You daren't tell because he may be threatening you, or saying it's your fault and you'll be punished; or you feel it's such an awful thing to happen that you couldn't tell anyone anyway.

Cheryl (in Chapter 8) was sexually abused by her stepfather until she was sixteen, when she decided to leave home. She told no one about it except her grandmother, who was sworn to secrecy. Looking back, both she and Ruth wish they'd been able to talk about their experiences sooner, but this had seemed impossible at the time. Hard as it may be, it's better to try and find a sympathetic person you could trust enough to tell than to continue to submit to something that may really mess up the way you feel about yourself, your family, and your future relationships.*

DIANE

Diane and her twin sister are sixteen and live with their parents. Their father has been unemployed for eight years apart from doing 'odd jobs'.

'My father has been an alcoholic for as long as I can remember and I guess I blame *all* my family problems on that. Everything he does annoys me and I hate being around him. He doesn't care about his appearance, and I'm ashamed of him. He has no teeth and no money for the dentist. He wears dirty clothes and has greasy hair; he smokes and always has reeking breath; he eats his dinner like a pig and then has bad indigestion afterwards. Every time he burps or hiccups I cringe, and every time he is in the toilet I put my earplugs in or turn my music up. You may have guessed my father disgusts me a bit.

But I love my father and I feel sorry for him, usually when my sister is nasty to him, as she is a lot, and he looks so rejected. But I didn't feel sorry for him when this happened: my mother told us we would receive £500 between us from the insurance company on our fifteenth birthday. I was looking forward to that money so

* There are also various places you can go for advice and help. These are listed in the Contacts section.

much. I was going to buy a bike at first, but then I decided on a hi-fi, since my old record-player was so old-fashioned – it was bought at an auction for £7. I was so proud that we were the first of our friends to receive such money to spend all on ourselves. We were cautious when the cheques arrived. My father had stolen money from our rooms before and denied it, so I hide money in the curtain seam, and he'd also stolen Mum's money from the post. As Mum found it hard to cash the cheques, Dad said he could do it and we've never seen the money since. It caused many fights and is still brought up when we fight. I was heartbroken. What could I tell my friends? I told them the truth, like I always have done; they all know about Dad and they are afraid of him. He knows people know about his drinking and he must feel very rejected underneath. But what about me? Am I not entitled to a better life? Or am I being selfish, should I accept the way things are? He doesn't give us anything on birthdays or at Christmas and I get so angry. Why does he have to spend so much money on drink and gambling and smoking? If he loves us, why couldn't he spare a little? In his case it would be the thought that counts, not the money.

We went on holiday to the USA to spend six weeks with a family, through a children's friendship project, and we came back a few weeks ago. I'd met people on the project and I knew I would see them again. I was so ashamed of my dad standing there in a cream-coloured 1970s suit with a toothless grin waiting for me to come off the coach. They all knew he was my dad when he hugged me. Then I smelled his alcohol breath, I went stiff and stopped smiling. Every time I come home from a holiday (which is always away from him) I half hope he will have changed. Maybe by a miracle he'd have become a Christian or something and stopped drinking; I would be so happy. But he never changes. I have little hope left and the tiny thread of love is beginning to break.'

SHELLEY

Shelley reckons there can't be many families like hers, although unfortunately there may be more than she thinks. She lives with her father and mother in the north-west of England, over the betting shop her father owns. Her father is an active member of the Territorial Army, which has always meant him being away on training programmes a lot of the time. Her mother has become an alcoholic, and there are frequent rows between her and Shelley's father, who is not a drinker himself. Her family experiences made her fall behind at school, but now, aged seventeen, she's at college taking a fashion design course that she really enjoys. She doesn't get on with her eighteen-year-old sister Valerie, who was always in trouble at home and at school. Valerie was thrown out by their father and now lives with her boyfriend and baby. Despite everything, Shelley is standing by her parents until she can afford to leave home.

'For my dad there's the office, which is work and his pride and joy; there's Territorial Army cadets, which is like a hobby but he does too much so it's like work as well; and there's me, as I do all the shopping and the cleaning and everything; and then there's Mum. She spends all his money, so she's last on his list. His priorities are completely wrong, but it's always been like that. My dad only thinks of money, the army and himself, and Mum only thinks of money, alcohol and herself. That's it really.

Mum hasn't been shopping for about four years; I have to do it. It's only about five minutes' walk to town, but she says she's got what people get when they're afraid to go out – agoraphobia. But at night she'll go to the pub. I don't see the difference really. I do all the housework – hoover, polish, wash, iron, cook. Everything. She shakes a lot because she's an alcoholic, and because she's got bad nerves. She hasn't worked since she got married. She doesn't do anything, and she gets up sometimes at about four o'clock. I used to be coming in from school and I'd wake her up, give her breakfast, but she doesn't eat a lot. About seven years ago she saw about six doctors and every one of them said she was going to die in a couple of years, but she's still going. She's gone very very slim, but she's got a big swollen stomach because she doesn't eat and she's got a wine gut. Her legs are just awful. Where people drink a normal glass of wine, she'll drink half a bottle to a bottle. I have to wash her hair and that now, as my dad broke her shoulder a month ago. She's had a leg broken, and her little finger's still broken because she wouldn't let them break it back, it's bent.

What will normally happen is my mum might get up at one, and have a glass of water with three nerve tablets, then she'll have a cup of coffee. She'll wait about half an hour and then she'll have a drink of wine. She'll have had about three glasses – not little dainty glasses like in a bar, I mean full lemonade glasses – by the time I come in. She never eats, and now my dad does the Sunday dinner and me and my dad both do normal tea. She only used to cook one meal a day, and that used to get her nerves very shaky. There'd be a row and my dad would say, "How much have you had to drink?" and she'd say, "Never mind how much I've had to drink," and then they'd just argue over anything.

Things that cause the arguments are stupid things like the tea isn't ready on time, or "You're ignoring me, Jim, you're watching the telly, talk to me." He goes, "What do you want me to talk about?" She'll go, "I don't care, just talk to me." He'll say, "I'm watching telly," and then it'll start. Dad will sit in the living room for half an hour and my mum will come in from the bedroom and bring the argument up again. Then when my dad's winning she'll walk out and come back an hour later and bring it up again, or something from a couple of months ago they were arguing about. Then she'll go away and come in again and in the end my dad's waiting for her to come in, you can see it; he'll be watching telly but he'll hear every noise and say, "Is that your mother?" and I have to go to the door and if she's halfway down the hall I have to turn her round and make her go back to bed. If I don't catch her she'll come in and my dad will flare up and batter her everywhere and she'll go, "Shelley! Shelley!" and I have to pick her up, wipe all her cuts and bruises and put her to bed, and calm my dad down, otherwise he'll get going again. I sit up sometimes waiting for him to go to sleep.

He's battered her that much that my mum's always threatening to knife him in his sleep. A couple of times he'll be lying on the couch watching a late film and he'll fall asleep but before he'll say, "Don't go to bed until after the film finishes," in case my mum comes in and knifes him! So I'm there ready to save the day. So he'll go to sleep and I'll watch the end of the film and then I'll go to bed. It's funny sometimes, laughing at it, but it's weird. It's because she provokes him really, but I still don't think he's got a right to hit her, I don't care what anyone says. He says, "She provokes me," and I say, "I don't care. *You* provoke *me*, do *I* hit *you*?" But it's my dad's fault because he was always away and she had no one. Before she got married she never touched drink; the only reason she went out drinking is because she got in with this woman who was about fifteen years older and an alcoholic.

When I was about nine I used to hate going to town with my mum. She'd go to the pub and we'd either wait outside or she'd send us to the cake shop, or ice-cream bar. I used to love that, but then again, it's bribery. It would be, "You can have an ice-cream while I go to the pub." It affected me at school too, my mum used to take me to school and leave me there, then at lunch time she'd come and take me home, so for the first two years at school I only had a year. When I was twelve I had a spelling age of seven. I go to night school for English now.

Everyone knows he batters her, but my mum's terrible. She'll go to the pub because she's got a black eye, for sympathy. It's terrible to say, but instead of staying in or putting make-up on to hide it she'll go out. And everyone will be going, "Oh, poor Barbara", and she loves that. But I can't stand people who say, "Well, she must enjoy it", because I know she doesn't. My dad says she must like it, but I don't stand for that and I've had rows with him over it. But he's got it from his dad, as his dad was very violent towards his mother. He must have watched his mum getting battered all the time. My nan used to hit my mum as well, and she says my nan's an alcoholic too, so I think it runs in the family each way. People always say you end up the same way as your parents, but oh God, if I see myself going like my mum . . . I reckon she'll die soon if she goes on too long.

Although my mum's not totally different when she's drunk, I've always said to her, "Mum, I hate you when you've got drink in you. But I love you when you haven't." When she's sober I can talk to her about anything. She knows everyone thinks she's an alcoholic but she won't admit it. About three years ago she went to a place for alcoholics, but she only went about four times. They were trying to dry her out, but she'd go there and then go to the pub afterwards. I know she's too far gone now to do anything. There's nothing more I can do. When I begged her to stop drinking she wouldn't; even when I threatened her she wouldn't.

My dad wouldn't consider going for help either. I think he's got a weird streak in him. I know it's common for men to batter their wives, but I think it's a sickness he's got. I help when I can now, but I don't get involved. I don't have respect for my dad when he hits my mum. I think of him as nothing. And when she's drunk I think of her as nothing. If I saw my mum in the street and she wasn't my mum, I'd ignore her, I'd think: that's disgusting, and the same with my dad. But I know I wouldn't be able to leave, not yet, not until I've got a job.

I never go short of money, but I think that's because he's guilty. Instead of, say, driving me somewhere, he'd rather give me a fiver for a taxi, he's just lazy. My mum's always been for me and my dad's always been for my sister. He loves her, she'll come down every week and he'll give her ten, twenty, thirty pounds and taxi fares. When we have an argument I say, "Do you care about me?" And he goes, "No I don't care about you, get out." I think he loves me but he doesn't like letting me know.

Once we got taken away, me and my sister. I was fourteen, she was going on sixteen. She was a trouble-causer. She'd stay out until about two in the morning, and Mum and Dad would be yelling and everything. One morning my dad was going on at her so much, and my mum was saying, "You hit me but you never hit her." So he went in and gave Valerie a black eye. The next day at school her mate went and told the teacher and there was a great uproar – "Oh my God, a battered child!" – and the police were round and all that. A social worker came round to the school and wouldn't let me go home. They took me to Valerie in her school. We had to stay with foster parents for two weeks, then we stayed with our grandparents.

My mum knew my dad was violent before she married him. He pushed her around a bit. I always say to her, "Why didn't you just get out?" She says, "Well, I loved him." I think; how can you love someone who hits you? I've learnt through the years to keep out of it, but I couldn't when he's hitting my mum, all three of us are fighting then. It's all on record. When my mum went down the hospital she always said she'd fallen downstairs, even though she hadn't. But one time, when we went, she broke her shoulder, her collarbone, and she turned round and said, "Yes, my husband done it." First time ever. I'm standing there thinking; great, carry on. The doctor said, "Do you want a social worker?" But as soon as my mum heard "social worker" – because of the last time, when we were taken away – she said "I don't want no social worker, go away!"

If they divorced it would be better really, but I've always said that I wouldn't know who to go with if they did. I know in the end

I'd have to get a job and look after my mum. I'd be better off on my own, I could look after myself but I'd only leave home when I'd got money enough to buy a nice house, because I've seen the way my sister was in this dingy flat, and I don't know how she stood it. I've always said: if I go out with a boy and he raises just one hand to me, that's it, finished. I'd never let my husband batter me. I'd batter him first! But my sister, she's grown up with my mum getting battered and now she's living with a fella and he's given her a hiding before now. When she was eight months pregnant he hit her and gave her a black eye. I said, "If he can hit you while you're pregnant he can hit you any time." She said, "Yes, but he's promised he won't hit me again." I said, "How do you know? You're as bad as Mum, saying you love him. How can you?"

I'm a terrible dreamer, I'll say, "What would you do if you had a thousand pounds?", and I'll tell a big story. First of all I'd get Mum sober. Then Dad would be nice. Then the house would be gorgeous, I'd change it all. But it's not going to happen. I've always wanted to change Mum and Dad, but I can't. There have been some times when the family has been happy. We do have a good laugh. My mum and dad will be sitting there, we just start messing, and I'll go and sit on my dad and pound on him. But that's only when I'm having a laugh, otherwise there's no laughs. I'm the only one who makes it a laugh. The last few Christmases it hasn't been happy.

If you looked in at our family, not knowing anything about us, you'd think we all loved each other. Dad will have a kiss and a cuddle with my mum, and he'll always kiss me good night. But if you lived with us you'd know. I know it's a terrible thing to say, but if my mum died I wouldn't miss her in the fact that she ever gives me anything. My dad will never change and my mum will just get worse. I've changed a lot. I'm frightened of my dad but if he did hit me, there'd be ructions then. My mum hits me, she'll slap me across the face, but she's so weak. I'd hit my dad back, but I'd never lay a finger on my mum, no matter what.'

JULIE

The street where seventeen-year-old Julie lives in a Midlands city with her parents and thirteen-year-old brother is full of relatives – her grandparents, aunt, uncle and cousins, and more around the corner. There have always been several houses to run between, and she and her cousins were more or less brought up together. This is great sometimes, but over-whelming at others. Her mother has worked since Julie and her brother were small, and currently has a job as a doctor's telephonist; her father is a sales manager. Her parents could not pursue their schooling, but are very keen for Julie to do so. She's doing A levels in English, economics and fashion, and has applied to do a university degree. All her life she has been very, very aware of her parents' expectations of her.

'I've always been encouraged to do well. By the time I was four I could play the recorder and read music; I really took to it. Then I was in the orchestra at junior school. One of my friends played the flute so I came home and said I wanted to play the flute too. I couldn't get lessons at school until the year after so they paid for me to have private lessons. I had a lot of pressure, like I had to take the grade exams every year. I got to grade five, and I had to take my theory straight away. The exam only came up twice a year. My mum said, "You enter for it." I said, "Mum, I haven't done any grade five theory yet." "Oh, that doesn't matter, just do a few test papers." So I did and I passed. I got ninety-two out of ninety-six. But the pressure was on to get that. I *had* to pass. You don't want to waste your parents' money. But I've stopped flute lessons now. I played with a flute orchestra at the School of Music and I wanted to give it up because I couldn't cope any more. I had a big argument over that. They said, "Why give up, you enjoy it, don't you?" I'd never enjoyed it really, but I did it for my mum's sake because she loved to see me going, and say, "My daughter plays in the flute orchestra." So she can be proud of me. She wants us to do everything they didn't do. I even stayed on at Brownies because it was important to my mum and dad, but I hated it for the last few years and I refused to go to Girl Guides.

When I said I didn't think I was going to do well in my A levels, they said, "If you're only going to get a C, why bother to do it, why don't you leave?" I have to get an A or a B or nothing. When I got my O levels I got five, and a CSE grade one, and they were proud of me. So they push me to get the high grades, but they push me so hard they make me think I'm going to get A's and then when you get a B you think, "I've failed", you think it isn't good enough. They push you like that: hints all the time. I feel a bit guilty, I always have this sense that I'm not doing quite well enough. Then you go through phases where you just can't be bothered to do anything, and you fail a test and it's total disaster.

My parents want me to go to university and I want to go now as well. But I know why I want to go for myself – I want to taste student life and be able to get a degree. But before, it was always a case of "Mum wants me to go", because she'd never had the chance. But they're not bad parents, they're wonderful parents really. It's just that Mum wants everything for me so much that I've got to work to get it. I don't know if I am actually doing all the things my mum never did. I do some things she did as well. But she failed her eleven-plus and left school at fifteen, so me staying on is a bit of a boost I suppose. My dad went to grammar school and I think he only got about three O levels, so he's pushing me as well. Sometimes I've rebelled against the pressure; I've stopped working and said, "I can't cope any more, that's it, I'm not doing anything else," and things about dropping out of school. But I don't think I ever meant it because I haven't got the guts to leave and I'm not ready for work. Mum and Dad are quite good about freedom and the times I can go out. I think they respect my judgement. There's jokes like "Oh, going out again", things like that, but they haven't stopped me so I'm quite lucky.

Mum pushes me more than my dad. I'm very much like him, we've got the same temperament. Although we clash a lot, I'm still closer to him in a way. But there are things you can talk about to your mum that you can't talk to your dad about, like girls' problems, even boyfriends. When I mumbled to my mum, "I'm going out with Tim," that was my first boyfriend and she got more excited than I did! But often I'll go and talk to my grandma if I'm having problems at school or something. I haven't got the guts to sit there and tell my mum, but Grandma will look at both sides of it; she'll help me out. My grandma knows everything, and she'll always understand. She's been through it before with my mum, so it's easier to talk to her. She's had a really deep part of my growing up. When we were little Mum used to work nights and Dad worked during the day, so I was passed over to Grandma and Grandad at night.

My grandparents' house has always been like a train station. I'll walk in and then as I walk out one of my cousins will walk in. My grandma loves having the children round all the time. Sometimes I won't go for about a week, and then I have to tell them everything I've done. If I want to escape from home I can just go to my grandma's for an hour and watch television, then I'll go back and I'm more relaxed, so I'm lucky really. If she wasn't there I don't know what I'd do, but then if she wasn't there perhaps I'd have had a different relationship with my parents anyway. I do get on with my mum and yet I don't a lot of the time. It's hard to describe. I can sit and talk to her about English, she's very keen on English. But things like when I was choosing my university, I applied to Ulster and I was worried they wouldn't approve. I was very worked up about it but all I got was, "Well, you'll be eighteen by then, so make your own decision, but don't expect me to come and visit you."

We're really close family, which is nice, but there's drawbacks as well. A lot of the time it feels a bit claustrophobic, so I appreciate my friends more now. I've spent so much time with my cousins, we used to go on holidays together, spend all year with them: Christmas together, Easter, birthdays, everything, like one big family. I've got a totally different set of friends now, more towny, and a lot of them have just got their parents, brother and sister, and that's it. It's quite hard for me to understand people who only see their cousins once or twice a year, and it's different when they have a family get-together. Like this Christmas it's the ten of us at my grandma's, but about twenty of us will go out for New Year.

I go through manic-depressive stages, perhaps because I can't just go and talk to my parents because they're generally quite busy and it depends what sort of mood they're in. But I'm the one with the violent moods: one minute I'm all right, the next minute – don't bother talking to me. But they'll argue with me, while my friends know when to stop. I have this complex about how awful I am at everything. I think if I do one thing wrong I'll never be able to do it again. I'm not as bad as I used to be, now I've got friends I can fall back on. They go through depressed phases as well when there's a test at school and we haven't revised. But I shake in exams, I get so worked up about them. I think probably my parents will push me as far as I'll go. When I stop they'll know they've pushed me far enough. It's hard to explain, but I always feel like they're pushing and pushing me and then when I stop they draw back and let me get on with it. Perhaps my mum does push me too hard on some things, but in a way perhaps that's good. Perhaps I need it. But she's pushed me so far too many times, and perhaps that's caused . . . not exactly a rift, but something in the back of my mind and I act on it. I shout things back but I don't know why I do it.'

RUTH

Ruth is a judo enthusiast and has been in several competitions. Until just over a year ago she used to live with her father who is a research chemist, her mother, a teacher, and her twenty-year-old brother. Now seventeen, she had started doing A levels at college but dropped out. For many years she was sexually abused by her older brother, always too intimidated by him to tell anyone about it. When it did finally come out, it was not done in a way that she would have liked; her parents didn't respond very supportively, and she left home. After several overdoses she is again living at home. Her brother is living and working elsewhere.

'When I was little I used to admire my brother. He used to be climbing into the playpen to get away from me because I'd be following him all the time! He used to get tantrums, and be quite violent and cruel. Just about anything would set him off. Like if I wanted to watch something on television, he'd go and turn it over, and I'd tell him to turn it back and he'd just go, "I'll give you a mouthful." He'd throw things at me and punch and kick me. I used to fight back, but he was bigger than me. It didn't stop me admiring him, though, because he was my big brother and I used to boast about him to all my mates. But after a while, it started getting to me. Once he really hurt me when he stamped on my ribs. I didn't say anything about it but I had a judo competition the next day, and somebody landed on me. I don't know if it was that or him that did it, but I cracked my ribs. I never told my mum and dad he'd done that. I used to tell them when he hit me, but it was always: "Stop aggravating him, then."

My brother started abusing me sexually when I was about seven, and he'd be about ten. It started out being cuddles in bed and just went on from there. He only had full sexual intercourse with me twice, the rest of the time it was just touching. I wasn't scared when I was little. I didn't know what was going on, I just accepted it. He used to frighten me and punch me to make me do what he wanted. He hurt me and said he was going to kill me. It just carried on, right up until I was fifteen. I was getting upset then and taking time off school. I told my judo coach, who told my parents, but they didn't really do anything. They said he'd got exams and they didn't want to say anything to upset him. But I don't think anybody said anything to him even after the exams. I don't think he knew that they knew, and I didn't tell him that they knew. I thought he'd get into trouble and I'd get into trouble too. I used to tell him I was going to tell somebody and he just used to laugh and say it was my fault so if I said anything, I'd be blamed. I did tell one of my girlfriends but she didn't know what to do.

I used to go to college at half-seven in the morning and I never used to get home until eleven at night. I went straight to judo and mucked about with the kids. I just didn't want to be at home. My brother hadn't actually hurt me for two or three months, but I thought if I went home and he was around it might start up again. My judo teacher asked me if I was having any hassles at home and I said yes, and he didn't say anything else. Then I was at college one day and the college counsellor got me out of class and told me that the judo teacher's wife had contacted the NSPCC and the police were coming round in the afternoon to take a statement from me. I was really upset. I wasn't expecting it then. At the time I wished they hadn't because I felt like everything was going wrong; I suppose now I'm quite glad.

I left home and went to stay with my judo teacher's family at first. I was angry at my parents because my brother was allowed to stay at home and I wasn't. It really upset me and I think that's partly why I don't want much to do with my mum and dad at the moment. I think my mum was very upset then. She used to ring me up and I wouldn't speak to her on the phone, and this made my dad really angry, and he said he was going to come round and take me home. But my social worker acted to sort it out, and they got a "place of safety" thing. At that time I wanted everyone to go away and leave me alone. I suppose I really wanted someone I could just be with, but I wasn't that close to anyone, although I got on really well with my judo teacher's family. They've treated me as if I was one of their kids, it's nice. I've got a key to their house and I could go round when I wanted. I used to just turn up and say, "Can I stay?" and they'd say, "Okay".

By the time I was sixteen I'd been living in all different places, and I also went in hospital when I took overdoses of paracetamol. The first time I was staying with some people I knew. They couldn't wake me up one day so they took me down the hospital. I was okay so they let me out but I took another one about a month after. I was at school when they found me; I had to go to the hospital and they pumped me out. Then I stayed in this place – it's called an assessment centre for under-eighteens. People go there who have taken overdoses or are pyromaniacal or have been in trouble with the police and they don't know what to do with them. It was terrible. They leave you alone all the time. They say there's somebody there if you ever want to talk, but they're always busy with outpatients. I used to get up about twelve and have dinner and have a meeting in the afternoon. In the evenings you're not allowed downstairs after nine o'clock, and you've got to be in bed by ten o'clock. I was there for six weeks. It was a bit of a waste of time really.

When I took the first overdose it was on impulse, I didn't mean it. The second one, I knew that I needed help but I didn't know how to ask for it. Then I took another one last August, and I was ill. I took about sixty paracetamol and I was sick every ten minutes for twenty-four hours. The police found me and took me to hospital and then they phoned my parents, who came and took me home. I wouldn't do it again. I've got sorted out a bit now, I've met some people from a kind of missionary thing. They're like Christians who go out on the streets and talk to people. I talk to them and they'll give help just because you need it, and they show they care about you in a different way. There's about ten of them – they're quite young, about nineteen or twenty.

I suppose what happened with my brother has affected how I feel about boys in a way. If they say: do you want to come back to my place? or something like that, I say yes, and don't even think about it when I don't know them properly or I don't even want anything to do with them. It depends, I just go through stages. I've not had any long-term relationships; I've slept with boys now and again but I didn't enjoy it, I didn't even want to do it

I think my parents expected too much of me over some things. Like they're both pretty intelligent, been to university and stuff like that. I was never that academic and whatever I did it wasn't quite good enough, like if I got a B, I should've got an A. My dad's really into science and he always wanted me to do O levels, and when I did CSEs he said, "That's all right, you'll get a grade one," but I got a grade two, and he said, "Oh, is that all?", and he wasn't joking. I used to pretend I didn't care, but it hurt a lot that they never said well done. They could've listened to me more and my dad could've cared about me more. I resented him for not showing any interest in what I did when I was younger, so even if he tried to be pleasant I wasn't always very pleasant back. In some ways they drove me away. I was always compared to other people. My brother was never that great at school, but he was dyslexic and they always made excuses for him.

I've never felt I could talk to my family. If I try to talk to my mum about anything she just puts on her teacher voice like I was one of her kids at school. I never got on with my dad. He was really moody and if he didn't want to talk to somebody he just sat down and wouldn't say anything, and if he did talk, then it was that everything's wrong. I was scared of him so I always did what I was told, and I still do because it's not worth the unpleasantness of his sulky moods. Now I'm living at home again I get on all right with my mum, but she's really smothering me. She wants to cuddle me all the time and touch me, but I can't stand that. I don't want anything to do with her because she should've been there when I needed her, and I don't think I've forgiven her. We chat about the weather but nothing more. I've never been able to talk to her about what happened, but I think my brother has.

I'd say to other people: don't just wait, don't keep it to yourself. If you think you need help, go yourself, or find somebody else and let them do it for you, because you'll feel better. Even if afterwards it doesn't work out right, it's better at the time, you'll feel you had control of the situation, whereas I didn't. I felt like everything was happening around me and I couldn't do anything to stop it. The counsellor I saw suggested writing down what happened and I tried to, but some of it I can't, I don't know how I feel about some things.

I've never been allowed to express my feelings, I don't know how to, and I keep a lot of them to myself because there's no one to share them with. I'm too scared to tell my parents how I feel about things. They don't understand why I took an overdose and I can't tell them because I don't want to hurt them. It feels painful because I can't show either of them what they're doing to themselves or to me. It's better now, I think I've become more tolerant of them and they're more tolerant of me. My dad's trying to show a bit of interest in some of the stuff I'm doing, which he never used to bother with, so I think they're trying to change.'

7

Family Fallout

A mother to her brothers: Jane
Piggy in the middle: Carolyn
Breaking up gently: Kate

In the traditional storybooks, it always seems to be father, mother and children, living happily ever after. But life has never been as simple as this, and some families stayed together in the past because it was impossible to separate, not just because they were happy. Divorce rates have spiralled in the last twenty years, as divorce has become easier to obtain and more accepted. Many children nowadays will have experienced their parents separating or divorcing before they reach the age of sixteen. A lot of you reading this will have been through it already. It's slightly different for everyone, because it depends on so many things, such as how old you are and how you get on with each parent; how they get on with each other; how much you see the parent who left; and whether either parent has got a new partner. It's very tricky ground, and there's often a lot of tension, pain and guilt around for a long time.

The effects that splitting up can have on children are complicated, but not necessarily all bad. The effects that staying together can have may be worse for everyone. Some parents do stick it out 'for the sake of the children', and in some cases this may provide children with a secure, two-parent childhood, but if your parents are visibly unhappy together, and arguing or fighting, it will rebound on everyone. It's quite easy to pick up their atmospheres and moods. Understandably, most children (particularly younger ones) would like their parents to stay together and be a happy family. Who wouldn't? In an ideal world, this is how it would be, but life's not always like that. Some girls recognised the conflict between their parents, like thirteen-year-old Samantha: 'If it wasn't for me and my brother and sister they'd separate or divorce. I feel it would be better sometimes as their arguing makes life intolerable.' Where there has been violence or drunkenness, it's often clear that life would be better with a separation,

Openness and communication are extremely important while all this is going on. Some parents think they can protect their children by keeping them in the dark about their plans to separate, and their reasons for doing so. This is rarely true; it can be even more upsetting not to know, and to start imagining lots of awful consequences. Then you may begin to feel guilty and to blame yourself for something that has nothing to do with you at all, as Jane describes. There are lots of emotions around, like anger, guilt and sorrow, which, if not talked about, get bottled up and can undermine confidence. Kate definitely felt it had helped enormously that her parents had always explained things to her and her brother when they were deciding to separate. Unfortunately, not all parents can do this if they are feeling hurt or angry, or if one parent just suddenly disappears off the scene, and this can make you feel very insecure. It may be difficult, too, to cope with the divided loyalties that may be involved – as Carolyn describes, when she had to act as a go-between for her parents. One girl whose parents didn't speak to each other wrote: 'I wanted to tell Mum what a good time I'd had with Dad but I thought it would make her feel bad as she didn't take me or my sister anywhere. I try not to speak to my mum about my dad and vice versa.'

Looking back, girls whose parents had split up often said they could see that their parents weren't right together, they wouldn't make each other happy and they wouldn't want them back together again now. As you get older you can see these things more clearly, and understand better the personalities and needs of your parents. There is positive fallout as well as negative, and some referred to the closer relationships they'd developed with one or both parents as a result: how they were enjoying greater independence and responsibility, or exploring new family relationships.

JANE

Fifteen-year-old Jane lives with her mother and two younger brothers – David, thirteen, and Simon, seven – and her mother's boyfriend, Martin, also stays occasionally. Jane's

*parents divorced a year ago. About eighteen months ago,
when they were in the process of splitting up, her father, a
physiotherapist in the air force was posted to Germany. Her
mother was drinking heavily at this time and there were a lot
of angry scenes. Her mother's job in the civil service involves
flexitime and weekend work, and for some time Jane had been
taking a large share of the responsibility for looking after her
younger brothers. This increased even more after the divorce,
and had inevitable repercussions on Jane and on their
relationship. Recently, however, she's been able to go out
more, and even has a part-time job in a hotel.*

'The divorce was all done on my mum's side from here. We were
out in Germany with Dad when he got the divorce petition last
year. He looked really upset and shocked. I cried and called Mum
everything under the sun. When I got home I wouldn't talk to her.
It was all dirty looks and bitchy remarks and David's hated her ever
since. I felt guilty directly afterwards. It was always "the children"
coming into it, so I thought: "Oh no, it's my fault." It was always
arguments about money problems and going out and leaving the
children. I felt if we weren't here they'd still be together. I got over
that after they both explained it to me. It hit Dad hard, he blamed
himself, then Mum was blaming herself. I left them to it in the
end. It was easier to block it out than sit there trying to work out
why. I felt like talking about it sometimes but I thought: they're
not going to understand. Anything that happened I'd blame the
divorce. I didn't want anything to do with my family. I didn't want
to live with Mum because it would upset Dad, and if I lived with
Dad it would upset Mum, and I didn't really want to live with my
grandparents because it would upset both Mum and Dad. I wanted
to be independent and leave everything behind and I thought
everything would be happy if I did that. I couldn't, of course,
because I was too young.

Because she'd divorced my dad I thought I'd never see him
again. I thought it was because of Martin and that's why I hated
her. I was horrible. I ignored her, called her names, I wouldn't
help her, I was really sarcastic to her. Unbelievable – I never
thought I had it in me, really nasty. It upset her too. In the end we
sat down and sorted it out. I said what I felt and she explained
where Martin stood and Dad stood, so I understood. We've got

used to Martin now, and he keeps Mum happy. There's a difference in her when he's here; we can talk to her about anything, and get anything out of her. I'd rather she had him and be happy; she's the nicest she's ever been now. She and Dad had argued all the time because he wouldn't spend a lot of time with her. When she found Martin she realised there was somebody else she got on really well with, so rather than stay with Dad and be unhappy and make him unhappy it was best to finish it.

It still upsets me now and then, but it's not too bad. I felt divided loyalties, especially when Dad came home, because although we live with Mum, she was cut out totally then. I thought she must feel horrible, but then Dad must feel horrible when he's not there. I felt really bad for both of them, and as if I wasn't giving either of them enough attention. When he comes home they try hard to be nice to each other, and Mum wishes it was like that when they were married. Dad came home last Sunday and then when Mum came home the boys ignored her. I go out in the kitchen with her so she's not left out and I think she appreciates it. She's nicer to me when Dad's home. It's also difficult to leave one to go to visit the other. Sometimes I wish that my parents were still together but a lot of the time it's better now they're apart because there aren't all the arguments between them. I didn't think we'd be able to survive with no dad. I thought we were going to be really deprived and dirty children.

I do most of the looking-after of my brothers because Mum does a lot of overtime. It started about two or three years ago, when I was about twelve and Dad was still with us. I was so young then and I wanted to be the big independent girl, and babysit to earn some money. They realised that I could do it, and it got more and more. I used to look after them about three times a week and all the time during holidays. At first I felt I couldn't handle it, it was a big responsibility thrown on me. I felt really awful because my best friend Sally was staying in as well with me and I got annoyed because she wouldn't understand that I had to do it. Then Mum came home and I got funny with her because of Sally being restricted with me. I'd get really nasty and sarcastic with her and wind her up. Mum went out a lot then until I got a bit frustrated and it all came out in an argument. It's better now, she stays in much more and arranges for the little one to go to a friend's house so I can go out as well. Because Mum's on her own she's got to prove to my dad and everybody that she can cope, so she's reluctant to let me out in case something happens to me. I think she fears she might lose custody of the boys or something.

I used to think I was being used, that Mum didn't care about us, and it came out in a really big argument last summer. When it all calmed down she said she was really pleased with what I was doing and that she couldn't manage if I wasn't doing it. When she says things like that it's all right. I'm a sister to the boys when my mum's here, but when she's not I'm like a sort of second mum, and sometimes this can be fun. I taught Simon to tell the time and he was really pleased, I felt as though I'd done something worthwhile just to see the look on his face. Then it has its bad points as well, like the washing and ironing; I mainly do my own washing. My school work suffered then. I used to go to school tired and break down in tears because I couldn't keep up, it was really horrible. This was mostly in the second year. Once I'd been crying and I explained to my tutor what was wrong and she said she'd pass a note round to my teachers to explain what was happening. So I didn't get too much hassle off them for not doing my work perfectly. They're understanding at school, they've been great. I never told Mum my homework was suffering. I felt I couldn't rely on her and if she'd been drinking you couldn't get decent answers out of her.

Mum was still with Dad when she was drinking. It was when she didn't know what to do about him, she was really mixed up. Her friend who'd been divorced used to drink as an escape and they'd sit and drink and she'd get drunk. It was an escape for Mum too, you felt she was trying to block you out, running away from her problems. It was mostly at the weekends, that was when the arguments came up; she could see me giving her these funny looks. She'd say, "What's the matter with you?" and I'd say, "Nothing", and just ignore the fact that she was drunk. She'd get really annoyed and once she started swearing at me and that was the biggest argument we'd ever had. She was saying I didn't deserve anything and I was stuck up. She was really being nasty. The next day she said she was sorry and she didn't mean it. It lasted until my grandfather, her dad, who's a psychiatrist, sat her down and she told him everything. He gave her some tablets to curb her drinking and he told me: if she looks as if she's about to drink too much see what you can do. It was difficult, we had to try really hard not to get annoyed with her, but we got her through it eventually, with

Martin's help. Now she hardly drinks at all, just a social brandy after a meal.

Mum used to hit me a bit too; she slapped me round the face three or four times, she'd get really screwed up sometimes. One day she came in, she'd been drinking, the boys had to go to bed and she hadn't made Simon's bed. I was doing that and she said, "Oh, you're so grown-up, aren't you, I wish I could be like you." I said, "Maybe one day you will, you'll grow up." She was trying to wind me up and I was winding her up back, and she hit me. I'd never dream of hitting my mum but just like a reflex action my hand came up and hit her. I looked at my hand and thought: What have I done! It wasn't like I'd hit her, my hand just moved. She was shocked, then she cried and she was really sorry and she hasn't hit me since. Now we talk it out and sort it out.

Dad's got a girlfriend now. He's really happy with her, and I'm glad he's not on his own. But I feel lonely sometimes because both my parents seem to have somebody, and my brothers are always together. Sally has a boyfriend, then there's just me in my little room. But I don't worry about it any more, I've got used to it. I find I can think straight when I'm on my own. I always find something to tidy up or to do to keep my mind off things I don't want to think about, so I'm not really lonely any more.

Looking back, I think if you think something then say it. I kept it bottled up and it was unbearable. I was so nasty and all my feelings came out in a big explosion. I'd sit and cry and tell Sally what had happened and she'd sort me out. Crying's the best way, and I felt much better afterwards. I think I understand people a lot more and I'll listen to people. I didn't think about anybody else before but now if somebody's got something to say, if they've got a problem, they'll come and speak to me. The divorce has made me much more responsible and independent. I'm more grown-up than other girls of my age. I did lose my self-confidence but I got it back. I used to think I was worthless and it was all my fault, but Sally helped me, she said I was looking at the bad things all the time.'

CAROLYN

Carolyn is an eighteen-year-old student nurse living in the nurses' quarters of a hospital near London. Her parents split up when she was fifteen, and her brother was seventeen. Her father left home and now lives with his girlfriend and their baby. Communication deteriorated between her parents soon after they separated, and Carolyn found herself passing messages from one to the other. Her brother had left home too, to go to university, so she felt even more abandoned. When she left school she got a job in a mental hospital and really enjoyed it, so she decided to train as a psychiatric nurse and hopes to work abroad for a while when she's finished her course.

'It all happened in the last three years. They had a once-a-year argument, but everything was fairly good. My mum had been working since I was eleven and she got a new job. At first it made life more interesting, but then she really got into it. She used to work late and go out with her friends from work, and suddenly she wasn't interested in my dad's job. It wasn't just with my dad, she wouldn't ask me or my brother how we were getting on at school. But I think it hit my dad more than anybody else, and in a way he was jealous because he'd been doing the same job for twenty-six years and he was really fed up. They started arguing and then for about a year they didn't talk to each other – well, they talked, but not really *talked*.

As soon as my brother and I had finished our exams, my dad announced he was leaving. It was a bit of a shock, but in a way I'd been expecting it. He and my mum were still talking then. Dad moved closer to London and got a flat. At first they got on quite well, and then they started getting really bitter. Everything was about giving money, like for me and my brother, or paying the mortgage. My brother moved to university and then my dad announced he was moving to Sheffield. That was when it really hit me, and it was horrifying. I'd lost my brother because he'd gone away, and now I was going to lose my dad as well! When they'd had arguments in the past, my mum would say, "That's it, I'm leaving, I'm going to get a flat," and I'd always imagined that if it happened it would be my dad, me and my brother together, and my mum would be somewhere else. But then when it did happen and my dad said, "You can come with me if you want to," I said, "I'm going to study at college, I can't leave now."

At this time they both used to spoil me rotten to make up for it, but it was a very difficult situation. I could say one thing to one of them and then I'd have to say it to the other one. You couldn't get them together. I've been like piggy in the middle. My mum would get me to ask my dad something, and I'd ask him and he'd say something, and I'd have to tell it back to her, and she would moan. All her anger would be taken out on me so I'd feel really bad. I remember one time we had a very high gas bill. My mum said, "I can't pay it, you'll have to get your dad to pay it." So I asked him and he said, "I've got my own bills to pay, I've got a flat, you'll have to ask her." So there's me trundling back again saying, "Dad's not going to pay it." In the end I had to practically phone Dad up in tears: "You've got to pay it, it's not fair, it's me who's stuck here." And then it was the same with the mortgage. My mum would tell me something conflicting with what my dad would say. I used to hear both sides of the story and I didn't want to hear either of them. I responded to both of them, but then I tried to block it out. In the end I said to my mum, "I don't want to know," and that's what I do now, I say, "If you've got something you want to say to Dad, you say it to him, don't get me involved." But at the time I didn't do that and in some ways I'm glad I was involved, because it could have got ten times worse. They could have been going to court arguing about bills and the mortgage and everything, whereas me doing it made it a lot easier. Things are more sorted out now.

When my dad was leaving he told me and my brother that he was going with his girlfriend, which I hadn't known anything about, and I was even more upset when he came back to see me a month later and told me that she was pregnant. I didn't know how to feel because I'd never met her. At the time my dad said he was going to tell my mum, but I was having quite a hard time with her. She was taking everything out on me, so I said, "No, don't tell her, I'll tell her." I talked to my brother about it and we both decided we'd tell her. But we just never got around to it. And now it must be about a year and a half since my dad told me and my mum knows nothing about it, she thinks he's living on his own. They're not even legally separated yet. It makes me feel really awful. But I think if she found out now it wouldn't be so bad as finding out a year ago. She's mellowed a lot, and she's got a boyfriend as well. At one point my brother wanted to tell her but I said, "You're not going to be at home, I am, and I'm going to get it all," and I said as soon as I moved away I'd tell her. But I didn't, because if she's really upset she's going to be on her own and I'd feel bad about that, she'd have no one to turn to. And I don't know if she'd really believe that the baby was his, because my dad had a vasectomy the year before, but he had it reversed. That's what completely threw me.

I'd always got on better with my dad before, I don't know why. Then although Mum put me under a lot of pressure I started getting on really well with her. We have our arguments but I get on better now with her than I did when I was at school. She just didn't seem to have the time for me then, whereas my dad always did. I've got further away from my dad. I was jealous of his girlfriend, and I felt shoved out of the way. She's about twenty-nine, my dad's about forty-six, so it's quite a big age difference. Dad wanted me to meet her and I said no. I was being very difficult. The first time we did meet I just ignored her. I think it's a fairly common reaction and I presume he felt upset as well, but he didn't let it show. He'd say, "You're on holiday, are you going to come up?" And I'd never go. But it's difficult to have contact because he doesn't really write and he couldn't phone me at home because of Mum. He phones me now here, and when I go and see him he makes a great fuss of me. The last time I went I got on really well with his girlfriend, she's nice, and it doesn't bother me so much now. I decided to be grown-up, and she must have noticed a big difference.

I don't feel guilty about them splitting up; the only thing I feel really guilty about is not telling my mum about him and what's going on. I wanted to see them back together at first, but after three months I didn't because I knew it would never be the same. But I'd love to see my parents talking, it would make it easier for everybody else to see them together. My brother said, "Say one of us gets married, it's going to be really awkward, especially if Dad's got a little child there!" But neither of us is likely to marry in the next ten years, and hopefully things will have changed by then.

I don't really think it's affected me much, but it's definitely made me more independent, more than I wanted to be then, and I was making all my own decisions. I was responsible for sorting the bills out and dealing with the financial side of things. My dad had always done it and Mum hadn't a clue. He also used to do a lot round the house: he did all the shopping, the ironing and the washing. Mum used to do the cleaning and tidying, and me and my brother would do our share. I did all the cooking because my mum used to work late. The one good thing about my family was that it was equal in terms of housework and things, like I'd cut the grass and my brother would be doing the ironing. But then suddenly I was doing *all* the cooking, the washing, the ironing and the shopping. But I think the worst part of it was being stuck in the middle and feeling responsibilities to both of them, feeling you've got to defend each of them, because neither were to blame, it wasn't as if either of them had run off with someone else. I did tend to stick up for him more than her, but there again I felt he was letting me down by going, so I became more loyal to my mum. Even now I've got mixed reactions, I don't really know how I feel.'

KATE

Kate, fourteen, and her fifteen-year-old brother, Neil, follow a complex rota system in dividing their time between their mother's house and their father's house. Their parents split up five years ago, when they were living in the house where their dad still lives now, with his new wife and her two sons. After they decided to separate, they all continued to live there until her mum found a suitable house round the corner. Her parents are still on good terms with one another, and Kate gets on well with both of them. Her dad owns a shop where Kate sometimes works on a Saturday morning or after school. While her mum is training to be a counsellor and does not have much money, her father is currently paying for most of their clothes.

'I was nine or so when it happened. I remember I was downstairs and had the cat on my lap. My brother was there as well. I think they told us that they weren't getting on very well. They didn't hate each other but they just didn't love each other any more and didn't get on like they used to, so they had decided to split up. I remember feeling a bit upset, but not badly. They didn't have massive shouting matches or hitting each other. I don't think I noticed anything, except Mum moved up to a separate room, but I don't know how long she was there for. I suppose I didn't think much of that at the time. I remember talking to my friend at school and saying that they might be getting divorced, but I don't remember being that worried about it.

We were close right through the divorce, so we weren't really upset; Mum and Dad were always talking to us about it all. Although they had arguments they didn't get us involved, they just sorted it out and it's worked out really well. Mum and Dad do occasionally have arguments now, but nothing bad. Now Mum's been doing a counselling course, so we talk about anything that's wrong. Neil has helped a lot and I talk to him if I'm upset or anything. I wouldn't have liked to have been through that with just me. It's good having a brother, even though I sometimes don't think so!

They didn't actually get divorced until a year or so ago. But divorce is only a word, it doesn't make much difference if you split up or get divorced. It's the same with Hazel and Dad getting married. It didn't really mean that much when they did get married the other week. They told us what was happening and talked to us and made sure that we knew they loved us; I suppose it must be different for other parents if they actually do hate each other. It would have been awful if I'd had to choose between living with my mum or my dad. I don't know what I would have done. I don't think I'd have been able to choose. It would have been easier if I'd have been told where I would be, but I wouldn't really have liked that at all and I'm sure my parents wouldn't either.

I think they jointly decided to get divorced, but they didn't leave straight away, it took quite a long time to find a house and it's lucky we found one so near. At Dad's house it used to be really quiet before Hazel and Steven and Patrick came. The house used to be always tidy and now it's always messy, and it can get pretty hectic. At first there were quite a few arguments, as my stepmother, Hazel, brought up Steven and Patrick in a totally different way to how Dad and Mum brought up me and Neil, she wasn't half as strict, but it's settled down now. Just sometimes I don't like them but we get on all right most of the time. Hazel's really nice and easy to get on with. I like her a lot.

My dad's house is not very far away, it just takes a couple of minutes to get there. We've got this rota, like last night I was round my dad's house and I stayed the night. Tonight I'm staying round my dad's house and tomorrow when I come back from school I'll come here and stay the night round here. Then on Tuesday I'll come back after school round Dad's house and then at seven I'll go round Mum's. It sounds really complicated but it's not. I've been doing this for four years now, so you get used to it. My brother does exactly the same as me. It occasionally changes if Dad or Mum has got something on and the other parent looks after you. It's not quite the same now because we can look after ourselves. I do like to know where I am, because you've got to take the right stuff. I suppose I'm a pretty organised person, so I like to know what I'm doing. We've both got two rooms, one in each house, so we spread all our stuff about. I wouldn't like to have one week at one house and then one at the other. I like to see my parents, especially my mum, as she hasn't got a boyfriend at the moment. I think she finds it quite hard sometimes, bringing up two of us.

My rooms are pretty similar in each house. I think I prefer my room round Dad's house because I decorated that and in the last couple of years I've got new furniture, but I also like my room at my mum's. Round Dad's I play loud music because it's a bigger house. I've got a stereo and record-player there and I've only got a tape recorder at Mum's. Patrick and Neil often have their friends round at Dad's so I don't like to go to bed too early in case anyone comes round, whereas here I go any time I want. I keep all my books round at Dad's house, but I bring them round here if I want to do homework. If I had a bigger desk here, I think I'd rather work here because it's quieter and easier to get on with it. It's really nice to have the house to myself sometimes; round Dad's that rarely happens. But if ever I'm bored I can usually find something to do round Dad's more than I can here. My friends come to both houses.

Luckily, Mum and Dad still get on well but there'd be absolutely no chance of them getting back together again. I think Hazel finds it quite difficult sometimes, although she and Mum get on reasonably well. They have to talk to each other about arrangements for us, so they have quite a lot of contact. I get on very well with Dad, we've got a close relationship, but I don't get time to talk to him much and sometimes he doesn't want to listen. I think it must be pretty hard for him. He's fairly open, especially for a bloke, and the other day I told him he was always saying he was tired, or it isn't his fault, making an excuse, and I was getting fed up with it. That was the first time I'd said that to him. Another thing is that me, Neil and Dad hardly ever spend time as a family, just us three. During the last holidays we three went up to London for a day and it was really nice. Sometimes I feel lonely if I'm round my dad's house and Neil and Patrick have gone out, I feel a bit left out. I'm fed up being the only girl round there. If I had a stepsister it would be different. Patrick and Steven and Hazel never seem like a family to me although they are, and I feel right being with them.

We've been a very close family. I think it's better to talk about your feelings, it's the way I've been brought up. I get on just as well with both parents. I suppose in a way it's slightly more open with Mum than Dad as I don't see as much of my dad because he's working a lot, and he's got his family to see to. Also I'd rather talk to my friend than my parents about boyfriends, and anything like sex and contraception, although my parents have always been very open about that. Sometimes I've needed to talk with her about little things I've been a bit upset by, like Dad's wedding, and that he recently had his vasectomy reversed, which probably means he and Hazel are going to have kids. Mind you, I'm really pleased because I like babies and it will be nice to have a brother or sister.

There wasn't anybody else that split my mum and dad up, and all the people Mum and Dad have met since, we've got on well with. I think them separating must have affected me, but not badly. I don't think I'm really insecure, like I think a lot of people would have been where it's been done differently. There are so many things that could have not worked out but they have. I'm glad they didn't carry on living with each other because it could have been a lot worse in the end. I think they chose the right time to break, before everything got really bad. Ideally I suppose I would have liked them to have stayed together, but there's no point if they're not going to get on. They don't still love each other. I think it's stupid that parents should stay together because of their children, but to some children it must be really important. They ought to try and work it out so it would be all right for the kids, not mess up their lives or their kids' lives.

It doesn't feel as if I'm living in a single-parent family, because I'm not. I've still got both parents and I see the same amount of both of them. I wouldn't like to live with my mum during the week and see my dad at weekends. We can go round Dad's by ourselves, we don't need a parent with us to drive us places. Sometimes I think I'd rather live in one place, like on Christmas Day. I wouldn't like to spend that day without seeing the other parent. It's times like that, and birthdays, and bringing my stuff to and fro. I must have wasted so much time doing that and bringing it all back again! But I would rather see both parents than just live in one house.

I think if you're going through your parents splitting up it's very important to talk to someone close to you about it. It must be really difficult if your parents don't talk to you. I think that was mainly why I was all right through it all, because my parents talked to us and we got on well with them, and talked to them as well. I think it would have been difficult if we didn't want them to get divorced and didn't want to live in two houses. I don't know what they would have done. It wasn't just organised and we had to put up with it or else. *We* had a decision as well. I'm sure we could have lived with one parent if we really wanted to, but I wouldn't have wanted to.'

8

Out On Your Own

After Mum died: Lisa
Can't take it any longer: Cheryl

There are different ways of feeling that you're out on your own.
You can be living with your family, or other relatives, and still feel
basically alone. This is how Lisa has been feeling since her mother
died and she left her stepfather's house to live with her elderly
grandfather. For her, the family ceased to exist with her mother's
death. She is trying not to think about the past, and feels it's now
up to her to make what she can of her life.

You can also pull up your roots and get totally out on your own.
When things get rough, it's very tempting to think about running
away, leaving home, getting away from everything and everyone.
Most young people have done it at least once, even if it was only
for an hour, or a day, or staying overnight with a friend. Others do
it more seriously, for days or weeks, and some even disappear and
don't return. You can leave home without your parents' permission
when you're eighteen, but before that, strictly speaking it's illegal,
although there's not in fact much that your parents can do about it.
If they really wanted to they could apply to the court to make you a
ward of court or put you into care, but this will be granted only if
you are thought to be in some kind of physical or moral danger.

Unfortunately, although it may be really bad at home, it can be
equally difficult trying to survive away from it. Thousands of young
people run away every year, and most find it very hard to exist on
their own. Paying for somewhere to live is a major obstacle, which
is why so many young runaways are either living in hostels or even
sleeping rough outside. Some people make out all right, but it's no
easy option.* For instance, Ellie (in Chapter 5) was ordered out of

* For information on where to get help if you run away from home or are
thinking of doing so, see the Contacts section.

the house after a massive row with her mother, but managed to find lodgings with a family, and then in a bedsit, before she eventually returned to live at home. Cheryl, however, has spent two years in hostels and squats. She'd already run away several times before life at home became too intolerable.

LISA

Lisa looks older than her seventeen years. She is at college in the north-east of England, training to be a hairdresser. Her parents got divorced when she was two, and her father took no interest in her until his next marriage broke up; by then she had no time for him. After her parents divorced she became very close to her mother, who led a fairly wild life and had lots of boyfriends until Lisa was about ten, when she met and married her second husband. Lisa hated her step-father and his young daughter, and there were lots of rows. After several miscarriages her mother and stepfather had her baby brother Edward, now aged five. Lisa was only thirteen when her mother was suddenly taken into hospital and died. It was awful living with her stepfather, and after an argument she left, eventually to live with her grandfather. She hasn't seen Edward for over three years; she feels basically that she is alone, and that her family really disappeared along with her mother.

'The happiest times were probably from when I was two until I was ten. After that it seemed to go downhill. I think it was because I didn't have to share Mum with anyone, and not having brothers and sisters I got all the attention I wanted. It was just perfect. I get a lot from Grandad now, but I don't really appreciate it. I don't mean it, but I can't help snapping at him. He irritates me because he's partially deaf and I have to repeat things all the time. We get on, though, and he never stops me doing anything. He doesn't say anything if I come in at nine o'clock in the morning as long as he knows I'm sensible. He's seventy-three but he doesn't look it, he's pretty spritely for his age. Grandma died when I was a few months old; all the women in our family seem to die young.

Mum had a blood clot on the lung. I was shocked when it

happened. All I remember is that she got taken to the hospital on Christmas Day, halfway through our Christmas dinner. She didn't get to eat her Christmas pudding. She was screaming upstairs, they must have been bad pains. An ambulance came, and the last time I saw her I was standing at the top of the stairs holding Edward and she was getting taken out on a stretcher. She gave us this awful stare. Three days later, when I was going to see her, my uncle came in crying. I asked him what was the matter, and his wife took me into the bedroom. She just sat me down and said, "Don't worry, Lisa, but your mum's just died."

I can't really remember much of what happened after that, it's all blurry. But I didn't believe it; I said, "She's died? What are you talking about?" She'd been in hospital loads of other times with miscarriages and one thing or another; I thought: why should this time be any different? I remember I phoned my best friend and said, "Guess what? My mum's just died." I couldn't understand why she was crying, it didn't really get through to me. I just got on with doing the rest of the housework and looking after Edward. Everybody else was crying their eyes out, the house was full of family. I even ate my tea that night. I think I was eating curry and watching the telly. Then I went to see her in the Chapel of Rest. That's when it hit me, because I'd actually seen her. I'll never forget that moment. I think my grandad and my stepdad were there. The veil was over her head in the coffin and the funeral director said, "Are you ready now?" I didn't know what to expect and I said, "Yes". Then he lifted it and I took one look and ran out down the street screaming my head off.

Before he married my mum, my stepdad used to buy me sweets to get round me. I never refused them, but it didn't change the fact that I hated him. It just made me ignore him so he'd think everything was all right. I hated my stepsister too, and I still do. She's an evil little bitch. She hated my mum. I think she was even glad when she died. I still hate the whole family, except Edward, and I think it's terrible for somebody of my age. I've never liked them even though we had a good life – good money coming in, and I had everything I could possibly want. I even had my own telephone in my room. We were planning a holiday but it never happened because my mum died and it spoiled everything.

When my mum was in hospital once, my stepdad had taken some dirty photographs of her friend, and I found them. In a way I'm glad I did but in another way I wish I hadn't. I've never seen anything like it. I kept them hidden from my mum for over a year, and it was eating me up. I used to get really mad every time I saw him. It was so frustrating not to tell her, but eventually she got to know and confronted him, and then chucked him out. But he came back, she always let him back. There was only one time when she was willing to go and I stopped her. I was just being selfish, thinking about moving schools and moving house. I still kick myself. I wish we'd gone now. I blame myself for making her stay. I know she didn't love him.

It's better living with my grandad than it was living with my stepdad. I'd never been totally comfortable in his company, but it was worse after my mum died. There was always something funny about him. He'd come up and put his arm round me, but it wasn't a fatherly thing, there was something else in it. And he'd burst into the room when I was in my knickers, and go, "Oh, sorry", have a good look and go out again. I'd be left feeling really awful. I asked for a lock on the door but he wouldn't give me one. I used to do all the cleaning. I was only thirteen, but I was like a little housewife. I looked after Edward. I seemed to be the one trying to keep everything together, and do my homework too.

A few months after my mum died, me and my stepdad had this massive argument. It all came to a head – I told him I knew what he was like. I called him a pervert, and a bastard. He used to cut out pictures of shoes and underwear, and had photos of Marti Kane in her skimpy dresses. I was getting really upset and angry, he was holding Edward and standing there with a half smile. I thought: there's something unhinged about him. He said, "Pack your bags and get out," and I said, "Fair enough, I can't wait to go. You disgust me!" I went to live with my grandad at first, but he thought he wouldn't be able to cope so I went to live with my auntie instead. It didn't work out. They were strict Catholics, and as you can imagine I'm not that sort of person. When they went to bed, I was going out! They'd led a really sheltered lifestyle, and their idea of a good time is to go to the library or something. I was there about two months, and then I came back to my grandad's. I thought the best thing to do was to see if I could live here because I was getting passed up and down like a parcel, and beginning to feel unwanted. I got depressed then, I hated myself. I tried to crash diet, make myself sick. I've always had a thing about my weight. I had no confidence at all. I've only just started to build it up now.

I hate Christmas Day since my mum died. It's not a happy time, it's one long miserable holiday. This Christmas I'm going to my best friend Helen's. I'm always over there, we're really close and she's been a real help to me. I feel comfortable with her family and I envy her. I don't feel I've got a family. I'm not close to my grandad. He tries to act like a moral father but I've never had a father, so what's he doing? I don't wish I had a dad; what you've never had you don't miss. I just get on and do what I like. I'm only seventeen so I'm going to enjoy myself and he can't stop me. He says he trusts me but I think he thinks I'm loose. He'd be terribly shocked if he knew I wasn't a virgin, but I would've told my mum, she had lots of boyfriends and she'd talk to me about sex. I've only been with one man. I've had chances with lots but it's not felt right. My grandad's always worrying about me but I look after myself; in fact, I feel as if I've been doing that all my life. I do rely on him heavily for money and I think he minds that, but when he's got it he gives it to me. He says he cares more about me than he did his own children. He's done loads for me all my life and sometimes I feel really guilty about it.

Everybody thinks I'm confident and really sure of myself, and I'm not. I think there's a different person on the outside to what there is on the inside. My grandad thinks I'm hard. I put up this front of being tough, that I don't hurt easy, but I do really. I've made my own defence mechanism. I think in a way that's good. It prepares you for life, makes you more independent. It's been hard from the word go, but I'd hate anybody to feel sorry for me. I was a really sensitive kid, but now nobody messes with me. I know I'd be a lot softer if my mum was still alive. I think sometimes people think I'll cling on to them because I haven't got anybody, so I'd rather not tell them at all. If they say, "Do you live with your parents?" I say "Yes," to save argument. I think with fellas, the younger ones back away. I find I get on better with the older ones so I try not to see anybody under twenty-three.

I think Mum knew I loved her, but I never actually told her. I was only thirteen and it's something you don't think about. But afterwards I thought: why didn't I tell her? Did she know that I loved me? It really got me. I used to hug her and say, "You're a lovely little mother," because she was small and skinny. I'd like to have had her there on my sixteenth birthday, because she always said she'd hire a place and have a big party for me. Of course it never happened. I think I'd also have been different in the way I looked at marriage. If she was here, I think I may have been more content to follow that line, but since she's not, I'm not going to get married. I'm going to push myself as far as I can. I think I've got more determination than I would have had if I'd always had someone to lean on.

I think you shouldn't dwell on the past. You've got to live each day as it comes. Occasionally I think about everything, but then you've just got to shut it out of your mind. It's too depressing. I'm not saying forget about it, I'm saying try to live with it. When my mum died, everybody was concentrating on the rest of the family. I think they assumed it didn't really affect me and they didn't know how to treat me. I didn't know how I wanted them to react either, it was a no-win situation. I think I got through it by myself. I've always been left on my own and I still feel I've got nobody. Each person is different on how long they grieve and how they grieve. I think with me being pretty young, I got over it pretty quick. Now I've started to try to pick myself back up again, and I'm going to try to build on what I've got!'

CHERYL

Eighteen-year-old Cheryl is delighted to be living in a flat in London, which she shares with Yvonne, who is five years older. After two years of living in various hostels and in a squat, she has finally got some space of her own. When she feels more together she might invite her mother to visit. Her mother was only seventeen when she became pregnant with Cheryl, but her father was already married and didn't stay around. Two years later her mother met the man who became Cheryl's stepfather. He is white like her mother; Cheryl's real father is black. Three more children – two girls, now aged eleven and seven, and a boy, now aged four – followed. Her stepfather works as a housing manager, and her mother as a secretary. There was always conflict between Cheryl and her stepfather, especially after he started abusing her both physically and sexually. At sixteen, having got her GCSEs, she could stand it no longer and left home. Over the last couple of years, as well as being on the breadline, living on £20 a week in the hostels and smoking forty cigarettes a day, she's tried out a number of jobs, working in offices, shops, pubs, etc. But her real love is drama and dance and she's been in several shows. Not long ago Cheryl sought out her real father, and is still getting to know him. Her boyfriend is soon coming out of prison, so at present her life is orientated towards that.

'My mum didn't live with my stepdad until she got pregnant; before that everything was me and her. I suppose I got spoilt really, no one else got a look-in. I'd had seven years on my own with her, and I felt pushed out of the way. My little sister was a daddy's girl; she was their first child. I didn't fit in at all, and I'd have rows. At first I hated her, I wanted to throw her out of the window. Then I started playing with her, and by the time she was seven she was really quick and I thought: this is all right. Then Gina came along and that was even better, then my little brother came along. I practically brought him up; I used to stay at home and look after him. I still miss him badly.

It was when my mum was pregnant that my stepdad started abusing me. I didn't want to tell her because I knew she loved him. I still haven't told her. I felt I was causing trouble just by being there, so when I hit sixteen I said, "I'm going." My mum asked me why and I just said, "Because I'm not getting on here." I'd run away from home about four times before that, and I knew my nan's door was always open to me. She knew the situation with my stepdad. I was only little but I'd made her put her hand on the Bible and promise not to tell. My mum's got about eight brothers and they're all big. I thought if she tells them they'll kill him. So I made her promise because it would hurt my mum and she'd end up hating me.

My stepdad abused me sexually and physically – by touching me, or he used to beat me when my mum wasn't there. First of all he was only hitting me; then I started hitting back and he didn't like it. In the end I was provoking him because I was getting sick of him beating me and I was getting cheeky and answering back. I wasn't going to get hit for nothing. When I started screaming he used to cover my mouth, and that's when he sexually abused me. My mum used to go to bingo in the evenings and I remember him making me touch him. I was only six. And when Mum was expecting Lucy it got worse, and then we moved and I just felt relief. When she got pregnant again I hated her because it happened again. She wondered why I was always rebelling against her and him, but I could never say anything, although I wanted to tell her.

He didn't actually have sexual intercourse, but he started putting things up me, like butter knives. It was quite painful and I'm afraid that I can't have kids because I did get pregnant and I had a miscarriage. My stepdad didn't stop abusing me until I left home. When I started saying no, he started hitting me; in the end I used to keep my mouth shut. When he was sexually abusing me I just used to lie there and think of my dance school. I used to think: I've got to get these steps right and do this and that. It's all I've ever concentrated on. It used to block out the pain. I don't know if it gave him pleasure or if it was just to be horrible, I didn't ask him. I bit him once, I don't know how he explained that to my mum. I wasn't exactly scared of him at fourteen, I don't know how to explain it. When I was with my friends I felt strong, but when it was just him and me I felt so small. There's this man and he's such a big person to you and you're supposed to love him and he's supposed to love you. He used to bribe me as well, and I would ask for things because I knew I could get away with it. It was yes, straight away, just to keep me happy. When I left home my mum said, "You're really ungrateful, he's spent so much money on you." Little did she know it was to buy me. But he wasn't getting away with it. I was using him in the end. I just hate the man. Whatever he says or does, even if he gave me all the money in the world, that would never make up for what he's done.

My nan knows why I left home and why I did what I did; she understood why I didn't want my mum told. She's young at heart, I can go to the pub and have a good laugh with her. But I messed up there, she got really fed up with me. I used to play music loud, go out with my friends, and come home different times of the morning because I wasn't allowed to do it before. In the end she suggested I went to Centrepoint Night Shelter, where they referred me to Alone in London. They put me in a short-stay hostel but I messed up there as well. When I left home I wanted to do what I wanted, I was just cheeky. Everyone has to have a turn at cooking, but when it was my turn I used to say, "No, I'm going out." And that's just not the sort of thing you can do in these places. I know that now. It doesn't work if people mess about. But at the time I was sixteen, I'd met my boyfriend when I was in the night shelter, and all that mattered was him, getting more money, and having a laugh

The night shelter is really horrible. You have to be there at five to eight in the evening to have your name put down, and they chuck you out at eight o'clock in the morning. There's a men's dormitory and a women's dormitory. Two showers, one for men, one for women. They cook meals for you, if you can call it a meal, plus a laundry service which ruined my clothes. But when you've got nowhere to go, you've got no alternative. You can stay there for up to a week, but I think you're only allowed three stays altogether. I've done my stays now. I can't go back ever again. The way they work it is if you stay there for a week and you haven't been bothering going to anywhere like the Advice Centre for help they say, "Look, you've had a week to sort something out. You're wasting our time and wasting our beds."

When I went there the first time that's what I was doing, just going out and enjoying myself. Once, when I was standing outside the night shelter, a pimp tried to pick me up. He goes, "I've got redskin [half-caste] girls working for me. Do you want to come and work for me, earn some good money?" I said, "Me? Who are you fooling?" He goes, "Come on, if you don't I'll end up beating you up and you won't be good for nothing." I just kicked him between the legs and ran round the back of the shelter and got in after ringing the bell for ages. The police eventually caught up with him, but these things do happen. Like I've seen junkies and alcoholics. I'll never touch heroin, coke or glue, Tippex or anything, petrol, gas, whatever. I smoke grass but I don't see that as a drug. I got offered drugs in the hostels, I even got offered crack. When you're in a place like that you do get a temptation to, but I think I'm a very strong-minded person. Nobody can tell me what to do.

At Christmas I went back to my nan's but I messed up again and moved into a squat. I was just seventeen. It was horrible, but there was me and my friends, and again nothing else mattered except having somewhere to live, food and company. You can't sign on the dole until you're eighteen, so I started thieving, just food. It was terrible, but that was the only way. Then I started going up the West End getting clothes out of shops. I found if I got good enough clothes I could sell them and make my money that way. I never got caught but I started thinking to myself: "What am I doing? I don't need to do this, I can work, I've got qualifications." So eventually I went back to Centrepoint again and tried to sort myself out. They referred me back to Alone in London and I went to a hostel where you could stay for up to a year. I had my own room, and eventually I would have got referred to a flat. But I was the only half-caste girl there and I got a lot of racial abuse so I left.

It was then I took it into my head to go and find my real dad. My nan gave me his old address; he wasn't there but I got the address of his work. It was a snooker hall and he was the caretaker. I thought: am I going to hate him on sight or am I going to love him? And all that went through my head was "Dad's not bad!" I'm still getting to know him. I like him but I can't say I love him. I don't think it would have bothered me if I hadn't found him. I think it was just one of those things in the back of my mind, especially when my stepdad started abusing me. I thought: if you were my real dad you wouldn't do that. I see him every week or two, but it doesn't bother me if he doesn't phone me. It's my mum that brought me up. You can have a thousand dads, but you can only have one mum. My mum's important to me.

Eventually I was referred to Centrepoint Bedsits and they offered me an interview and that's how I came here. But now I've got my flat I feel I've got nothing else to fight for. When I left home I knew what I wanted was my own place. Now I feel so lazy, like I haven't got a goal any more.

When I was going through the abuse, I thought: why is it me? But then I met girls in hostels who'd been through the same thing and it was like a relief that I wasn't the only one, and I wasn't evil. He used to say I was evil, and that if I told my mum she wouldn't believe me and she'd have me put in a home. Most girls blame themselves, but I don't. I've never had any counselling because I've come to terms with what happened. I know it wasn't my fault. When I talk to the other girls that have been through the same thing, that's like counselling in itself.

The advice I'd give to girls who were abused like I was is to go to Social Services because they can help, not do it like I did it, go from hostel to hostel. I'd advise them to go to counselling, and tell their mum if it was their dad who was abusing them, or their dad if it was their mum abusing them. But I can't take that risk. When all that Cleveland stuff came up about kids getting abused, I wanted to tell someone about me, but I was afraid that if it went to Social Services they would try and take Mum's kids away. I could never do that to her or my sisters. My little sister says my mum's proud of me now I've got my own place, and she doesn't have to worry about me any more.

Leaving home is one thing I'll never regret. It's the best thing I've ever done. The only thing I maybe do regret is not seeing my little sisters growing up. And I miss Sunday dinners and going to the park, but I had to put up a front to enjoy these things. I'd be a liar, though, if I said there weren't happy times at home, and on holidays, and when my sisters were born. But it was more relief than excitement; the abuse would stop for a little while. Then it would start up again. I used to pray that my stepdad would leave, I'd provoke a row to see if he'd go. Once I heard my mum downstairs crying about two o'clock in the morning. I went down and asked what was wrong and she said, "I just can't take you two any more. I'll end up leaving one day." That was just about the time I decided to leave, I realised what it was doing to her. As it is now I can't tell my mum, but maybe if they split up I could say, "Right, this is why I left home." Maybe she thinks it's her? I miss them all. I think about them every day. I got in touch with my mum three days ago, after six months, because it was my little sister's birthday. She was asking if she could come and see me, but I didn't want her to just yet.

I don't know how I feel about my mum now. I know I love her a lot. I don't talk to her for months on end, but if anything happened to her I'd crack up. I know she loves me. My little sister told me that when I left home my mum was crying and she didn't sleep or eat. I never knew this before. I always thought my mum was just for my stepdad and her kids and that was it. I would like to spend time with her on our own, so she could get to know the real me and I could get to know her better. All I want from my mum is for her to tell me about my dad, and for her to start seeing me like an adult, not as a little girl. Then maybe we'll become friends so that I can tell her anything I want. Sometimes I think I hate my mum for not noticing what my stepdad did. Sometimes I think she does know and she's not doing anything. Then I think: no, don't be stupid. I don't think she could choose between me and him, and it wouldn't be fair to ask her to. Maybe before the abuse it wasn't perfect, but I had my holidays, I went to a good school, I had lovely clothes. I had a normal childhood apart from the other side. If it wasn't for him, I might not have had all that. Mum might not have had the beautiful home she's got. She might not have three beautiful kids. I wouldn't want her to end up regretting what she's got because of what he's done to me. It was him that drove me out, not my mum or my sisters.

I don't advise anyone to run away, but if that's the only way you can do it, it's got to be done. But find yourself somewhere before you leave home. It might take you a couple of days to find a hostel or something, and then just go. If you can't tell anyone you want to leave, then just go and when you get there, phone them. There are places, like Alone in London, who help you sort out what benefits you can get, even though you're under eighteen. You don't have to sleep on the street, there's always somewhere you can go to get help. My first few stays I was just dossing. I'd advise anyone who goes in there: don't doss, don't take it as a holiday because it ain't. You don't mess the workers up or your friends, you only mess yourself up. It's taken me two years because I messed about so much.

My boyfriend's in prison and my life's revolving around him at the minute. I met him two years ago at the night shelter. His dad's from Nigeria, like mine. I told him about my stepdad, because at first I didn't like him touching me at all, so I just blurted it all out and I wouldn't let him move until I'd finished. He said, "I'm nothing like him. I'm not going to do anything like that." I've stayed faithful for two years, and I'm waiting till he comes out before having my fun. I've got eighteen-year-old friends and they're going clubbing and that, but I've seen more than they'll ever see. I've grown up faster than they have. I've been through more than they'll be going through in the next ten years. But now I can laugh in their faces. My nan's really proud of me, and my mum's happy now that I've settled down. This place is what I've been waiting for and I'm not going to mess it up now.'

Since this time, Centrepoint Night Shelter has moved to a new location with better conditions.

9

Choose
Your Partner

Pleased to be gay: Maria
Arranging the marriage: Pardeep

Do you feel free to choose the person you have a relationship with? Or the person whom you may spend the rest of your life with? As you may have already experienced, parents can get quite concerned when it comes to your friends, especially boyfriends. They usually make it very clear who they think is good for you and who isn't, and their views may be quite different from yours. It's not always easy to work out why you are attracted to people, whether they are of the same or the opposite sex. Luckily we don't all fancy the same sort of people. Most people are assumed to be attracted to the opposite sex; if you prefer the company of the same sex it does not necessarily mean that you're gay or lesbian, but it may be so. I don't think that people are necessarily born with a certain fixed sexual inclination, but rather that this may develop and change. Understanding your own sexuality and sexual identity can be confusing enough at any time, but in your teens it comes together with lots of other discoveries about what sort of person you are.

If you think you might be a lesbian, it's hard to know whom to confide in. Parents are not an immediate choice; sex is often a tricky and embarrassing subject for them and accepting boyfriends can cause trouble enough. On the other hand, they may try to be more understanding than you expect, like Maria's father. Although homosexuality has been more open and accepted since the sixties, the way sexuality is often portrayed, especially in the media, is aggressively heterosexual. In school, children are only too quick to apply their own put-down labels, and these include 'poofter' and

111

'lezzie'. There are a significant number of gay and lesbian teenagers around today, but it takes a lot of self-confidence to declare it. In the 1970s people talked about the right to express their own sexuality, but sadly, in the 1980s there has been a general narrowing of attitudes, and the spread of AIDS (Acquired Immune Deficiency Syndrome) has contributed to myths and prejudice against homosexuality. This limits our personal freedom and makes girls like Maria and her friend afraid to enjoy their love for one another openly.*

Western culture idealises romance and the process of spontaneously falling in love, whether it be with someone of the opposite sex or the same sex. In some other cultures – such as Asian, Turkish, Arab and other Muslim societies – finding a partner is more formally organised. Parents are responsible for arranging a good marriage for their daughters and sons, and this system is still preserved by many such families living in this country. Marriages are usually arranged with the son's or daughter's happiness in mind, and intended for the mutual benefit of all families concerned. Some girls accept and approve of this while others, who have grown up here, may feel very resentful, wanting the relative freedom to go out and meet boys and ultimately choose their own husband, like other girls of the same age. They may also find that any success in education is helping them more towards a better marriage than a future career. Some families who have lived here many years have modified traditional behaviour and allow their teenage daughters to wear modern fashions, jewellery and make-up. They may, however, still arrange marriages for them. In Chapter 2, Destine describes the problems of her sister's arranged marriage, while in this chapter Pardeep describes how an arranged marriage now seems preferable to choosing her own partner.

MARIA

Maria lives with her father in the north of England. Her parents are separated but still live in the same area, and her two younger brothers live with her mother. Maria is sixteen and in the fifth year of an all-girls High School. Although her

* See the Contacts section for organisations that give information and advice on being gay or lesbian.

*father suddenly had to adapt to the responsibility for a
thirteen-year-old daughter, they get on well and have a fairly
open relationship. However, Maria didn't feel she could tell
him that she'd discovered she was gay and was having a
relationship with her girlfriend. He was to find this out when
she wrote to me and left her letter on the word-processor disc.
But instead of hitting the roof as she'd feared, he took it quite
calmly and in some ways she is not sorry that this happened.
Telling her mother is a different story: they don't get on well,
and Maria definitely does not want her to know that she is a
lesbian.*

'My parents are separated and live about ten miles apart. I live
with my father, my two brothers live with my mother. My mother
left my father about two-and-a-half years ago because she felt life
with him could no longer continue and they would both get on
better separated. I was asked who I wished to stay with and I chose
to stay with my father. He is now going out with a girl who lives
close to us who is twenty-six years old. I think she's a nice girl and
though my mother detests her through jealousy and others con-
demn her younger years, I stand by them because I don't feel there
should be anyone who decides who you go out with except
yourselves.

When my parents separated it was a great shock to me. I had
grown up with the continual arguing so it had become part of my
life and I didn't expect there to be anything else. When my mother
and my brothers left, the house was suddenly very quiet. I began
to miss them terribly and I became depressed; my grades at school
dropped and I argued a lot with my friends and also my father, who
was left with the responsibility of caring for a daughter he hadn't
actually noticed before.

My father found this difficult. He didn't really understand what I
needed, but he made a conscious effort to learn how my mind
worked. He is a civil engineer and is quite clever and well brought
up. He expects the very best from me, which has taken a while for
me to get used to. He pushes me at school, makes sure almost
every minute I have is used effectively – which is all very well in
his world, but in the mind of a sixteen-year-old they must be
allowed flexibility and freedom. My friends dislike my father for
the very regimented lifestyle he leads and it can mess up my social

life, but I know he does what he thinks is best for me. I don't argue as much as I used to with him. We can talk relatively openly with each other, yet there is a lot I keep from my father.

My mother is altogether different. She has recently been diagnosed as having multiple sclerosis and she gets very ratty and moody, which I'm ashamed to say I have no patience for. I don't get on wonderfully well with her. She is always trying to persuade me into buying feminine clothes, which really irritates me. Surely it's my decision what I wear! However, I do worry about her MS. I don't know much about it and the ignorance worries me. I have been told that she has had MS now for about seventeen years and ever since she's known she has been worse, but before she was almost fine.

I'm a relatively happy, outgoing person. I am ambitious and hope to do well. I am quite bright (modesty for you!) but I don't push myself enough. I'm quite popular with a large circle of friends and a few close friends, so I am lucky. A lot of people would love to be like me and I try to make the most of what I can. I get on really well with my brothers. When I lived with them we argued and fought like cat and dog, but now I only see them about once a fortnight we get on much better.

I have been gay now for about nine months. I got drunk whilst on a school skiing trip. I was staying in a room of four with a girl I knew was gay and in my drunken state I went with her. I don't mean just because I went with a girl I think I'm gay, it just took an event like that to help me understand that my feelings for people I knew and had known were more than a strong friendship. I strongly believe in what I'm doing and it is hard to imagine my life any other way. I've read lots of books on the subject of whether gays are born or made and I believe I was always this way. I can remember incidents as far back as infant school which being gay account for. I also feel a lot more people in this world are gay but are hesitant at accepting themselves because of the fear that no one else will accept them.

I told my close friends when I returned off the skiing trip what had happened. Most of them helped me sort out the confusion about myself and now I know what I am they have all accepted me. Four of my semi-close friends have come to me since I told them and talked to me, saying they feel they might be gay. I feel if it wasn't for the prejudice against gay people there would be many more people in the world who'd be able to come out of their shell and talk and behave freely as homosexuals.

My mother and the rest of my family don't know, as far as I can tell. My father found out by reading this manuscript, which I had put on a computer disc and hidden. He found it, so he now knows everything. He came to me and told me he knew and told me he was anxious that I didn't put a label on what I am and put it down to a phase I was going through. I don't mind him reading the disc, as I know I would have done the same if I was him. He hasn't stopped me from seeing my girlfriend and I don't think he would tell her parents, but he has stopped her from staying at my house for the night (she used to sleep in my room!). I am glad in a way that he knows what I'm thinking, but only because he has taken it quite well and not hit the roof. I don't think this is any phase. I want to take life as it comes but I must admit that I do want to have children – I might end up adopting them or something.

I am at the moment going out with a girl who has been a very close friend of mine for four years. She approached me about six months ago saying that she thought there was a possibility she was gay. I had to be careful what I said, even though I fancied her; I didn't want to influence her. So I talked to her to try to help her. I took her to gay pubs and nightclubs which I very occasionally visit, and listened to what she had to say. I eventually told her what I felt and she asked me out. That was three months ago. About six weeks ago she finished with me. Despite the fact that she said it didn't matter to her who knew, except her mother, she decided she couldn't continue going out with me as too many people knew. I was devastated, mainly because I could do nothing about it, so I had to accept that she didn't want me any more, which was hard because I did – and still do – care an awful lot about her. Anyway, about one month ago she asked me back out and I said yes. She told me she had been confused about our relationship, didn't know how to handle people knowing, and wanted to try to get away, but now she doesn't mind or care who knows as long as her family or mine don't find out. She was very upset when my father found out and now won't go near him because he scares her.

I think I love my girlfriend and she says she thinks she loves me. I enjoy spending time with her and miss her when I don't see her. I walk round with her hand in hand and kiss her in public, but usually at night because most people think I'm a boy. We also "see each other" at school. One day someone will see us and recognise us, but as long as my mother and her mother don't find out, we don't care.'

PARDEEP

Pardeep is taking a theatre arts course at school in Yorkshire. She is fifteen and lives with her parents, one sister (twenty) and a brother (twenty-three). Her eldest sister is married and has moved away. Her parents came to England from India in the mid seventies with the two eldest children and set up a clothing shop. She and her sister were subsequently born here. Her father recently went back to India to visit her grandmother, and also with a view to setting up a business there so that he and Pardeep's mother can move back. Pardeep is looking forward to his return as family life, which is always rather complicated, is not so nice without him. Her mother has to work even harder than usual and her brother is throwing his weight around. There is perpetual conflict because her sister has a boyfriend, and this rebounds on Pardeep's life. She keenly feels the contradictions between her life at home and that with her friends, and also the way her brother is treated compared to her and her sister.

'My oldest sister had an arranged marriage, and they want us all to have one. They think they can look for the boy, make sure he's got a good job and a reasonable family, nice to talk to and that. My other sister's got a boyfriend, Joe, who's half-English and half-Indian, and she says she's happy with him. My parents don't approve of him, so she's having a really hard time. He used to be my brother's friend; she's been going out with him for two-and-a-half years, but my parents only found out nine months ago.

It's affected the way my sister gets on with my parents. They don't treat her the way she used to be treated. They turn nasty against her, and they're turning nasty against me now because I stick up for her. I say she should be allowed out, and then I get shouted at, so I'm in the middle. I think it's partly because Joe's half-white. People talk about his dad because he married a white person and my dad doesn't want people to talk about us like that.

Also they think he isn't good enough for my sister because he hasn't got a steady job. They don't think he'll be able to support her. If she got married to him she'd have to work. But he's got his own market stall where he sells jackets and on a Saturday he can do about £1,000 in one day, but they don't see it like that. She said, "You can't stop me. I love him and I want to marry him!" They plan that as soon as they've found a house they're going to get engaged. Once they're married she'll go and live with him, but until then she's staying at home.

Although my parents may get used to it I don't think they'll ever accept it, and if she married Joe she won't get as much as we will, because when you're married you get a certain amount of gold and clothes and whatever. She says it's fair enough and as long as she's happy she doesn't need anything else. She's done a beautician's course and she's thinking of opening up a salon, but if she did my parents wouldn't really help her, it would have to be her boyfriend who helps her. But they just bought my brother a new car, and they bought him the shop. He's forever getting money off them and my sister doesn't get anything. She's treated worse than the dogs because she chooses who she wants to marry. In a way it's like buying people. They give my brother so much so he'll do what they say. But my sister doesn't want to be bought, she wants them to accept her the way she is, and at the moment they don't.

I sometimes go out with my sister and Joe, but my parents – especially my mum – resent me enjoying myself with them, because at the moment my mum's cutting my sister off. Joe used to be allowed round once a week but now she doesn't even like him coming in. My brother's taken over my dad's role in the family in that when there's been festivals that Dad plays a role in, he's had to do them. But also he thinks because my dad's not here he can say that Joe can't come into the house. My mum doesn't really say anything because she doesn't want to hurt my brother, she gets really upset because she doesn't know what to do. Every time Joe phones up, it's awful if my brother picks up the phone. He'll say my sister's not in or something.

My brother's got girlfriends but because he's a boy my parents think it's all right. When he went out with this white girl, they were a bit funny about it, but they didn't really mind. I don't think it's fair. Just because we can have the babies it's like we've got to stay in and not be allowed out until we're married. They let me out to parties now, but I've got to put up a big fight about it. They say I can go out when I want, but it's only that they know I don't go out much anyway. After school I'm really tired so I tend to stay in most of the time. I did go to a party on Saturday, but I had to warn them two weeks before for that. When I ask if I can go to a party my sister says, "Let her go out, it's only a party," and my mum goes, "No, she'll end up like you."

My sisters and brother were allowed to go to parties, so it's backfired on me, and if I get a boyfriend they'll be really hurt. I do go out with boys, but I just have to keep it secret. If my parents don't approve, I can't help that: it's the way they've been brought up. But I've been brought up very different. I don't really like to lie to them, but I don't go out with lads just to get at my parents, I'll go out with them because I like them. I know it's not right, but I think I should be allowed to live my life the way I feel and not how people tell me. The worst thing was when a friend phoned up whose house I'd said I was going to, but I wasn't really, so I had to make up another lie and then I got deeper and deeper into it. I don't know what they'd do if they found out. But my parents don't seem to trust me. It's awful not to be trusted, especially by your own family, because you feel as though everything you do you're being watched. They think that as soon as I say I'm going out, I'm meeting a boy. I'll come home and they'll say, "Where have you been? You only went to the shop, how come you've taken so long?" It's awful.

My parents think I should learn the Indian language and dress like them when I go out, and when there's any Indian functions I've got to go and be all Indian and talk to aunties that I hardly know. Then when I go to school and out with my friends, I dress the way I want. It's like being split in half, doing this for them and this for me. I just like to be me, but it's hard with parents like mine. But although it doesn't sound like it, in a way my parents give me a lot of freedom. There are girls I know that aren't allowed out at night, and not even allowed to talk to boys in the street. Although my parents are both Hindu, they're not really strict about religion, just as long as we don't go out with boys, or smoke! My brother's allowed to drink and smoke, and they don't mind my sister and I drinking with the family, but they just don't like us going out and drinking. I think in a way they're trying to be as open

118

as they can, but they find it hard. They try to be modern, but their modern and ours are completely different.

Before my dad went to India, and before my eldest sister got married, every Sunday morning we'd all come down and have breakfast together. Then we'd just sit there and talk about relatives, and about what we're doing, where we're going, things like that. It was really relaxing and it used to make me feel secure. It was something I looked forward to. And we used to watch videos; Mum would make popcorn and if she was in a good mood she'd start telling jokes that no one found funny, but everyone laughed because it was so stupid. It used to bring us all together. As soon as my dad went, it's like something really big's gone. A big chunk of our lives disappeared.

There's times when I get really fed up. I just end up going into my room and crying all night. I can't talk to my sister because if I'm not allowed to do something, she'll say, "Just do it, I did." But I don't want to go behind their backs and do things. I feel quite lonely, and I've always got to have people around me because I feel really insecure. Maybe Mum's shouted at me and I've gone upstairs really upset. I think: why can't she understand the way I feel? I have anger and sympathy and everything mixed up inside, it's awful. It's all trapped up there and I think of the books I've read, and I've never read anything about emotions. I think if someone talked about them, to see how other people feel – that it's not just one person who ever feels like that – I think it would be good.

After seeing the way my sister's been treated I think I would like an arranged marriage to stay on the good side of my parents. My sister can't see it but in a way my parents are just thinking of her, seeing that she gets a nice boy and nice family background and everything, there's security there. But she wants Joe, so they're going to have to live with that. They told me it's up to me when I want to get married, but I want to get married fairly early, eighteen or so, so that I can have children so that my parents get to know their grandchildren. By the end of next year they'll be looking for a boy for me. It sounds unusual but if you've been brought up that way it's fairly natural. Parents find you a boy through word of mouth, and then you meet them. You don't have to say yes straight away, you get to go out once or twice, to get to know them. If you think it's a possibility your parents will discuss it and then you get married.

I'd like to have been able to talk openly with my mum, but it's just impossible. There's been times when I'll walk in and say something, dropping a big hint, and she'll just change the subject. She's never said anything about sex or contraception because she doesn't think I go out with boys. I think out of both my parents I get on better with my dad, but no way would I be able to talk to him about anything like that. I'm closest to my sister, but she doesn't really take me seriously enough. My parents and I used to be fairly close, but ever since they found out about Joe it's been more like two sides – my mum, dad and brother on one side and me and my sister on the other.'

10
What's Normal Anyway?

Brought up by Dad: Tina and Joanne
Alternate weeks, alternate homes: Karen and Amy

Can anyone still paint a picture of a 'normal' family as father, mother and children, living happily ever after? Certainly not, as a quick count of any street or school classroom will prove. Your experiences, too, show that family life is extremely varied. There are obviously families like this, but there are also plenty of stepfamilies and single-parent families, and some other less usual forms as well, such as communes and lesbian families. Whether they're living happily is something that varies across them all, and ever after is a long time. If families split up, it's more usual for children to stay with their mother, but not always so, and the number of single-father families has been slowly increasing over the years. Tina and Joanne talk about living in just such a family, being brought up by their dad.

Having to cope with life in one home may seem different enough, but what would you do if you had two? What address would you put in your diary, or on your passport? It may sound weird, but this is not so uncommon either. Some parents who have split up have solved the custody question by living near one another and dividing the weeks so that their children spend about the same amount of time with each. There's usually some rota system whereby it's clear in advance where they'll be on any particular day. It may involve a block of time like a whole week at each place, or a more complex arrangement, but it's one that rarely changes, so that you'd know, for instance, if it's Wednesday then you're at Mum's house. Kate and her brother (in Chapter 7) had this kind of arrangement. It clearly makes life more complicated, as you have to shift certain things from one place to the other all the time. But it's a good way of spending time with both parents regularly and equally and becomes just a normal way of life, as Karen and Amy describe.

TINA AND JOANNE

Sixteen-year-old Tina and thirteen-year-old Joanne have been brought up by their father for most of their lives. Their mother remarried and lives about fifty miles away; she works as a secretary. They live on the south coast of England with their dad and their brothers Nick (fourteen) and Terry (seven). Their father has been married three times, so they also have two older sisters from his first marriage. Terry came from the third marriage, which finished a few years ago. Tina and Joanne's parents split up when they were five and two respectively, and their father got custody of them, Nick, and their eldest stepsister, who was about fifteen. He was then a freelance musician. Life had changed radically, but it was to change even more when their father was hit by a drunken driver, resulting in two broken legs, a fractured skull and multiple other injuries. He took several years to recover and their eldest sister helped to look after them. She's now married and lives close by with her two children. Their father's leg would heal and then break every time the plaster was removed. Microsurgery was recommended, but gangrene developed and unfortunately the leg had to be amputated. Eleven years after the accident, they are still waiting for the insurance settlement. Throughout this time, their father has been at home looking after them. He has had to make ends meet on state allowances, and money has been very tight.

Tina

'I don't think my mum could have minded my dad having us otherwise she'd have got us, because at that time they weren't that keen on letting single fathers have custody. I get on with my mum now a lot better than I did. I think I used to hold a bit of a grudge subconsciously against her for not wanting us with her when she left, and not trying hard to have us. I thought she should have helped more to bring us up. She's never given us any maintenance money and we didn't have enough support because of that. She said that every few months she'd buy us clothes but she only did that for one year and that was three years ago. What she does now is put money each month into a bank account for us. We think it's about a £1 a week for the others and for me about £6 a month because I'm older.

Our elder sister looked after us for the first few years. She was fifteen, hadn't got long left at school and didn't want to go into a job. Dad was going in and out of hospital having different operations, he'd broken just about everything and they reckon he actually died for a minute! It doesn't seem a different sort of childhood, but other people think it's different. And some people get queasy about blood, but I've seen blood and gangrene and I've seen my dad's leg when it's been cleaned and he's had new dressings on it. I suppose it did bring me and my dad closer together. It's only been the last couple of years that we've had fights – all families have fights, though, and we're no different.

Over the last five years my dad's taken against me changing the way I look. First of all it was just me wearing black; he said I had to wear more colours. Then I started dyeing my hair and he complained about that. I wasn't really intending to dye it in the first place but I got one of those wash-in things and it went wrong. It went purple with silver streaks in. I wanted to keep it that colour but Dad made me dye it black. Then he got very annoyed in the summer holidays last year when I was totally bald both sides. He doesn't stop me, but he says it's going to prevent me from getting a decent job.

Money was a bit of a struggle when we were younger. At first, because spaghetti was quite cheap, we were having that every meal. Little kids complain about having the same thing every day but you can get dye to turn food red and green and pink, so we had silly colours to make it more interesting. Dad couldn't afford much more. Just after they broke up it wasn't too bad, but then he had the accident and he hasn't worked since then except for a bit of voluntary work. I think he gets about £78 a week and a disabled car. When I was doing a Saturday job, quite often I'd have to lend him some money because he couldn't afford to get things, like a pair of shoes for the others. I was getting about £7, working just mornings or afternoons, washing up or clearing tables. He usually wanted to borrow about £10 but he gave it back the next week. That's why I wanted to leave school straight away and get a job. But my dad said I had to get more exam passes. There were two exams I failed and I'm taking them again this year.

Sometimes I get on with Joanne, other times I can't speak to her at all. When we were younger we shared a bedroom and we always used to argue about silly little things. I got a bit annoyed when she started to wear black and change her hair just because I did. I've gone out to be different and then everyone else starts doing it. But I'm the only girl round here who's got DMs and wears a leather jacket as well. It's my dad's jacket at the moment – I haven't enough money to get my own!

My stepmother, Anne, was only around for three or four years, from when I was about eight. When she was actually staying here I didn't like her that much, but I get on with her all right now. She kept complaining that Dad favoured me and Joanne, which he didn't, he treated us all the same. She used to really favour Nick and Terry, but she wouldn't admit it. Dad seemed a lot happier at first with her, and that's why I didn't say anything about it. I was quite pleased when she went, but I wasn't for the others because they'd got quite attached to her. I don't think I ever got really attached to anyone.

I don't think it makes any difference whether it's the mother or the father that brings you up. If they know how to handle children and if they want to look after them, they can bring them up just as good. One of my friends has been brought up by her mother and she's more or less the same as me. She's a lot more embarrassed about talking about things like periods and that to her mum than I was talking to my dad. It didn't really bother me, it's just something you've got to say something about. If I've got anything to talk about I talk about it to both my mum and my dad. I can't talk to my dad about sex or contraception, I'd just be really embarrassed, although I think my mum gets even more embarrassed. I've got the Pill at the moment for my periods, but Dad knows I'm on it.

A lot of people who are in two-parent families seem to think you're lower-class than them because you're in a one-parent family. I just turn round and say, "From what I've heard of your family life, it's no happier than we are." Some of the arguments the kids at school have with their parents I know I wouldn't have with my dad.

He treats us all about the same; he hasn't got any different rules for any of us. Some parents don't want to look after their children, they want to go out. Dad's only gone out for the last three or four years, but he didn't go out for ages, other than when he used to go down to Anne's or she used to come here. So we've never had to be minded, my sister's the only other person who's looked after us.'

Joanne

'I was only told about two years ago that my mum didn't fight for us and I didn't ever want to go up there again. I always made an excuse not to go, but now I don't mind so much. I haven't ever said anything to her about it. Mum and Dad only see each other when Mum brings us back, but they get on quite well. Tina goes up to see my mum a lot more times than me. When all three of us go up there, me and Nick usually go out and Tina goes to town with my mum.

I don't think my mum could cope with all three of us living with her and I don't think she'd be able to handle us now we're older. I think Dad enjoys it. I don't talk to my mother as much as I do my dad. I feel closest to my dad, although I don't talk to him about my boyfriends, I usually just talk to my friends about that, and I don't talk much to Tina. Dad never really talked to us about personal things, and Mum's not the sort of person who talks about anything like that.

Tina didn't get on very well with Anne, my stepmother, and it might be because she'd spent more time with my mum and didn't like the idea of someone else trying to look after her. I liked Anne a lot, I wish she was still here. She was really good with us, and I have quite a special relationship with her. I think it's better than with my mum. I quite often see her because when Terry goes to see her I go with him.

Dad gives us pocket money, but we only get it if we do our jobs round the house. It's not too bad, we divide the housework between us. Dad usually does the cooking but sometimes we do it if he's not in, and he does quite a lot of cleaning. Nick's jobs aren't any different to ours. He has to do his own room and hoover upstairs and that. I usually get about £2 pocket money and £1 for dinner money. And I get another £1 for walking the dog three times a week. And we get a bit of pocket money when we go and see our mum.

People like to call us punks and gothics and I have a lot of arguments with my dad, usually about my clothes or my hair. I don't think I've ever argued about who I go around with, and only occasionally about going out, but we have to be in at a reasonable time anyway: school nights at nine, and Saturdays about half-ten or eleven. He's strictest on what time we have to be in and where we're going. If he doesn't want us to go somewhere he says, "You can't go!" There's no negotiation, we go somewhere else. I suppose I get enough freedom, because with both a mother and a father you'd have to ask both of them and they might disagree, but with Dad it's either yes or no. He worries about us, but he doesn't really confide in us. I think he may confide in my eldest sister. Most of my friends like my dad. They think he's really good for staying with us and looking after us for all these years. I do too, and I think I know him better than a lot of other girls know their dads.'

KAREN AND AMY

Karen and Amy are sisters. Karen is eighteen and Amy is fifteen. Their parents split up about ten years ago and their mother still lives in the same house with Chris, whom she's been having a relationship with since the separation. Their father has no such permanent relationship, but shares a house with his sister. At first Karen and Amy saw him only at weekends, when he would collect them from school in a taxi, take them off to another part of the city, and drop them back home again two days later; but after two years this all changed when he bought a house round the corner from theirs. This seems like a perfectly natural solution as, like Kate (in Chapter 7), they spend time with both parents in two homes that are very close to one another.

Karen

'Sundays come and go and it seems like a normal Sunday but at seven o'clock we get ready and go to Dad's from Mum's, or to Mum's from Dad's. I'm in my second year of A levels and I have a load of books to cart round and massive folders to bring from one house to the other. I feel I'm complaining about such trivialities but it takes up most of the day! I've got a million Sainsbury's bags, and they split and it's really embarrassing, especially if you've got dirty washing or something! Most of the time I take the car and it's only about five yards away! You've got to load it up and unload it the other end, then take the car back. I have to take all the clothes that I wear in a typical week and then there's my tape-recorder. I practically end up taking everything except the ornaments! If I've left something at one house I can't think straight because I know I'll need it and it will be at a crucial moment. It's okay though. I do my work wherever I am, but recently I've found I work better at my dad's because I've got a bigger room there, and also he's always looking over my shoulder to make sure I'm doing the right amount of work a day.

I definitely feel there's a different ethos when I'm at my mum's and when I'm at my dad's. I feel equally comfortable in one house as I do in the other, but for different reasons. They're very different houses – my dad's house isn't fully furnished, there are floorboards everywhere and plaster hanging off the walls; I think that's what I like about it. I like places that aren't perfect and I see Mum's house as more perfect in comparison. I eat a lot more at Dad's, and I also find it easier for my friends to be round there because I've got a bigger room and they can all sleep there. Maybe round here at Mum's I feel more in a homely mood, whereas round there I feel it's a lot livelier. We've also a dog and two cats there. I feel easier here if I wanted a boy to stay over, my mum would let him. Round there, I suppose I could, but I never have. And round here I can smoke, whereas to my dad, I've never said anything about it. And I'd never talk to him about sex or going on the Pill, I'd tell my mum all of these. In that sense I feel a lot closer to my mum. I think I know a lot more about her life than I do about my dad's. Like if he's going out I never ask him where or who he's going with. We do talk about things but we talk generally, or have mild arguments or lively discussions. I don't love one any less than the other one. I think I enjoy their company in different ways.

I don't remember anything about them being together. I only remember my dad leaving. It's been quite normal living with Chris, and I didn't feel resentful of him. But I was older and I understood that they weren't going to get back together again and I feel a lot better that Mum has got someone she can be with. I wish that my dad had a steady too, but I think he can look after himself. I sometimes wonder how I'll feel when my mum and dad get old, because I tend to feel guilty about things like that. I think Mum and Chris are bound to stay together, so I'm not really worried about them so much.

I'm probably lucky I have a setup like I do. I get on better with my parents than a lot of my friends because we're not all under the same roof for too long. I suppose the worst thing about it is that my mum and dad don't talk, and I'd be amazed if they ever spoke to each other again. My mum would, but my dad's stuck in his ways. If anything needs to be sorted out she'll write to him and he'll tell me and I'll tell Mum. It's funny that Amy and I don't talk about it with them, I'm really complacent about it. I don't think I even know the full story of why they split up. It doesn't seem important, it's all in the past. I don't really mind why it happened as long as they're happy in the life they lead now. I'd never want them to get back together.

Mum and Dad have different ways of going about things, like he doesn't ask me where I'm going, because he knows I'm not that stupid to walk home from the West End on my own at four in the morning. Mum's more concerned, but not in a domineering way. She wants to know when I'm coming back, who I'm going with and where I'm going, but because she doesn't tell me what to do I don't mind telling her. It makes me feel a lot more responsible to be trusted. I think from an early age I had the privilege of being trusted a lot more by my parents than some of my friends have been. But I prefer to tell my mum and dad where I'm going. I don't feel I've got anything to hide.

I find the thought of living in a nuclear family funny in a way – the image of it puts me off. I wouldn't want to live in that situation. I'm not opposed to it, but I suppose I can't imagine living in one house all the time. I think I'd hate it. I think the best thing about having two homes is that sometimes you need a break from one house. I don't understand how people can stand being in the same house the whole year round when you can come to a different house and get rid of the conflicts you might have had in one house. I don't know a lot about living on your own but I think them paying half for each thing and not having us for a week helps financially, and also if we're getting annoying at least they know that by Sunday we'll be gone! Sometimes on a Sunday when I'm at one house I look forward to going to the other, not because I want to get away from that house but it's like a new event. And it's good having two phone numbers, and two cars – as long as I don't forget what address I've put on something!

I think all my friends know where I'm going to be, but they know if they phone one place and I'm not there I'll be round here. I come round here a couple of times a week to get something or to see how Mum is, and I go round to my dad's a couple of times too when I'm here. I'm proud of my family, the way they are, and I'm proud of the way we live. It's a topic of conversation too – if I need to talk to someone incredibly boring and they say "Who do you live with?" I say, "Well, this is what happens . . ." and I go on and on. I used to be quite ashamed of it but now I'm really proud of it. I feel like everyone else is not normal having parents that live together – why don't *they* move from each house each week? I'm quite shocked that they think it's weird. I see it as so normal.'

Amy

'It's fine living as we do; a week is long enough to settle down but short enough so you don't have too much of one parent. I don't go and stay at the other house midweek, it would ruin my psychological routine. But if I'm round one house and I want to be at the other, I just go round for the evening or just an hour or so. If I need some help on my history homework, my dad's very good, but if I'm really depressed then I have to come to my mum or talk to my sister. It's a real female and male thing – Mum listens to your problems, Dad helps with your homework! I think my mum's a pretty reasonable parent and some things I can talk about with her that I can't with my dad. I'm his daughter, I don't want him to know I'm going with boyfriends. I don't think I could take anyone home to him. I can take ordinary friends there, boys and girls, but it's like a friendly room, not a relationship room. Both our houses are completely different. My room here is like a hippy dosshouse and round Dad's it's all colour-schemed and I've made it how I want it. That's the room I like to relax in. I used to feel totally different in each house but I think that's got a bit less. I think I'm just me now.

Mum told me the other day that when Dad walked out Karen

took me to the bathroom and said, "You've got to be really nice to Mummy now because she's going through a very hard time." She's always been a responsible sister. She waits up for me quite a lot; sometimes she's more concerned than my parents are. I think as she's my sister she should be on my side, and she's not. She says, "Amy, how long have you spent on the telephone? You know you're only allowed half an hour." But when I'm at my dad's and I go out I like it that she takes the job of being concerned about me. So if I don't fight my mum I can fight my sister!

I think Chris and I get on better now. I used to resent him a lot, and I don't feel I can make as many excuses for him as I can for my dad. Sometimes I used to say, "He's not my dad, he can't tell me what to do!" But he really does love us and treats us like we're his, and he likes having us here. I know my mum's in love with him, so I might as well accept it. He's a really nice person so it's all right, but what gets embarrassing is like when we had a parents' evening at school and Mum and Chris came. Chris had helped me with my drawing, and my art teacher said, "That's probably where Amy gets it from." It's things like that, and they must be a fairly common occurrence for the teachers, but not for me, and it makes you want to die!

I think compared with a lot of my friends I've got really cool parents, but like Karen I find it embarrassing that they don't talk. When I'm walking along with my mum, and my dad walks down the street, I don't know what to do. He's never asked us how we feel about it, and I hate that. I wanted my parents to get back together all through primary school and in the first and second years of secondary school, because all my friends had parents together. But in the third year I changed. I think about ten girls in my class haven't got parents together and about five of them don't even know who their dad is. The people I'm meeting now, one of their questions is, "Are your parents still together?" It's quite a trendy thing! I think it's made me grow up a lot. I think kids in a nuclear family seem to be far more naive about the world, but I also think a lot of people whose parents are still together seem more secure. I think I'm always going to be insecure about the relationships I have, and especially my relationships with boys, because one of the most important relationships in my life – my parents' – has ended on me. But I'm pleased my parents are the way they are because Mum's really happy now, and I know they wouldn't be happy together. It's a bit of a hassle having to pack your stuff every week, and if anyone phones you have to say, "I'm at my mum's next week." But other than that it's all right. My parents have always been fair, saying that we can choose to stay with whoever we want. But they're totally different people and it's totally equal, so I could never make the choice between going here or there.'

Open Endings . . .

Life moves fast, and I'm sure that within a short time of speaking to me, some of these girls' lives will have changed radically. Families are not static. Likewise the emotions and relationships within them ebb and flow, and people develop and change in the process of becoming adult. The girls who have spoken here will inevitably move on, but their feelings and experiences will be repeated endlessly in other families and in other ways. Each has given us an intimate – and sometimes painful – glimpse into the heart of family life today.

Useful Contacts

Many of the places listed below will give you information about where to go for advice in your local area.

Anorexia

Eating Disorders Association, Sackville Place, 44 Magdalen Street, Norwich, Norfolk NR3 1JE. Tel: 0603 621414

Contraception; pregnancy testing; advice and help on abortion

Brook Advisory Centres, 153a East Street, London SE17 2SD. Tel: 071 708 1234
Specifically for young people. Ring for details of local centres.

Death

CRUSE – Bereavement Care, 126 Sheen Road, Richmond, TW9 1UR. Tel: 081 940 4818
Gives advice and help to anyone, of whatever age, who has lost a close relative. In some areas, groups have been set up specifically for children and young people. Ring for details of local branches.

Depression, loneliness or suicide

Samaritans. Tel: 0753 32713 (Office hours only)
Look in your telephone directory or call the above number to find your local branch, which runs a 24-hour service.

Lesbian and Gay advice

Lesbian and Gay Switchboard, BM Switchboard, London WC1N 3XX. Tel: 071 837 7324

Can also put you in touch with organisations that help young lesbian and gay people 'come out' to their parents.

Lesbian Line, BM Box 1514, London WC1N 3XX. Tel: 071 251 6911

General family problems

National Association of Young People's Counselling and Advisory Services (NAYPCAS), 17–23 Albion Street, Leicester LE1 6GD. Write for details of local counselling services.

The National Children's Home (NCH) have twelve Carelines over the country, including two in Scotland and one in Wales, for counselling, advice and help. Call the London number (081 514 1177) to find your nearest Careline.
There are two projects which specialise in youth counselling in the west of England, called SHARE. These are based in Taunton (Tel: 0823 277133) and Gloucester (Tel: 0452 411428).

SOCIAL SERVICES DEPARTMENTS

Local social services are listed in the telephone directory.

Leaving home/running away

Alone in London Service, 188 King's Cross Road, London WC1X 9DE. Tel: 071 278 4224

HOUSING AID CENTRES can be found in many towns and cities. They will put you in touch with places that cater more specifically for young people. Look them up in the telephone book or ring the main office of Shelter (071 253 0202) for details of local branches.

Other useful agencies to consult are Citizen's Advice Bureaux (CABs), which are listed in the telephone directory, or NAYPCAS (see **General family problems**).

One-parent families

National Council for One-Parent Families, 255 Kentish Town Road, London NW5 2LX. Tel: 071 267 1361

USEFUL CONTACTS

Rights and general legal issues

Children's Legal Centre, 20 Compton Terrace, London N1 2UN.
Tel: 071 359 6251

CITIZEN'S ADVICE BUREAUX (listed in local telephone directories).

Sexual abuse and violence at home

Childline, Freefone 0800 1111
Free 24-hour national help and advice service for children and young people.

The National Society for the Prevention of Cruelty to Children (NSPCC) have a 24-hour helpline: 071 404 4447. They will give advice and can refer you to somewhere for help. This number is in London, but they will call you back if necessary, or you can reverse the charges (a Freefone national number is planned). Or you can ring your local NSPCC branch, in many parts of England, Wales and Northern Ireland. Scotland has a separate system, called The Royal Scottish Society for the Prevention of Cruelty to Children (RSSPCC). Call 031 312 6452 (Edinburgh) or 041 556 1156/7/8 (Glasgow) for advice, or information on somewhere nearer you that can help.